Mrs. Charles E. Joiner
1806 Raa Av.
Tallahassee, FL 32303-4418

Be Your Own Caterer

Trudy Cannon

Be Your Own Caterer

Macmillan Publishing Co., Inc.
New York
Collier Macmillan Publishers
London

Macmillan Publishing Co., Inc.
866 Third Avenue, New York, N.Y. 10022
Collier Macmillan Canada, Ltd.
First Printing 1975
Printed in the United States of America

Library of Congress Cataloging in Publication Data
Cannon, Trudy.
    Be your own caterer.

    Includes index.
    1. Dinners and dining. 2. Buffets. 3. Menus.
4. Entertaining. I. Title.
TX737.C27   641.5'4   75-15702
ISBN 0-02-521150-1

To John, with love

CONTENTS

Foreword   ix

Introduction

1. Your Kitchen and Basic Utensils   3
2. Tips for Entertaining   6

Part I. Sit-Down Dinners

3. Simple Dinners   19
4. Gourmet Dinners   42
5. Elegant Gourmet Dinners   58

Part II. Informal Entertaining

6. How to Run a Buffet Party   81
7. Fork-Only Buffet Dinners   85
8. Knife-and-Fork Buffet Dinners   120
9. Very Special Entertaining and the Brunch Party   160
10. Soup, Salad, and Dessert Luncheons   173
11. Homemade Bread and Hot Biscuits   183
12. Sauces and Salad Dressings   186

Index   195

FOREWORD

To me, a well-cooked meal is as creative as an artist's painting or a dress designer's new fashion image. I plan my dinners with an eye to color, texture, and the size and shape of foods. I take great pride in serving great foods. People are wondrous to behold when given foods they enjoy. Whenever people tell me they are "just a meat and potato fan," I am tempted to sit them down, blindfold them, and then give them foods they would never dream of eating. My guess is that they would change their minds about what they like to eat.

To me, cooking well has meant having to go to school and study with the great chefs and cooks in Europe and New York. I learned the excitement of experimenting with foods and recipes. I learned never to be afraid of trying a new recipe—if you can read, you can cook. I learned never to panic—and I learned never to lose my sense of humor.

To me, cooking well means learning to plan ahead. The well-prepared hostess is the relaxed hostess. If you design a menu that can be prepared largely in advance, you will be fresh and unworried on the day of the party. The hostess who has every detail under control—from food to flowers to seating arrangements—can afford to enjoy her own party.

Don't look for spectacular foods in this book. I have sought, instead, unusual menus which you can use or adapt to produce great dinners successfully on your own. Try always to visualize your meal as a whole, well ahead of preparing it: Will the foods complement each other? Will the colors and shapes look attractive together? Is the balance between rich and plain a good one? It is this kind of unobtrusive planning that distinguishes the superior hostess—that makes the guests exclaim, "That was a perfect meal!"

In this book, all the sit-down dinners are planned for a basic eight—you can halve or double the recipes as needed. The book progresses from simple dinners in the first chapters to more elaborate meals in the later chapters, but nothing is included that is too difficult for the cook with zest and imagination to accomplish. Gourmet cooking is good cooking—not fancy, spectacular food. In each menu, however simple, I have tried to include one famous dish—whether it is an appetizer, salad, entrée, or dessert. In the last part of the book, I suggest menus for buffet entertaining and for unusual entertaining—from The Hero Sandwich Cocktail Party to The Brunch Party.

My aim in writing this book is to show you how easy it is to be your own caterer. With imagination and careful planning, you can serve delicious and noteworthy dinners, with or without outside help. Above all, I hope to persuade you to think of cooking as fun, as a joyous, creative occupation that can be as fascinating for you as it is rewarding for your guests.

Introduction

1

Your Kitchen and Basic Utensils

Modern kitchens are designed to save space and to be time- and labor-saving. But whether your kitchen is large or small, very push-button modern or just adequate, you will get out of it—cookingwise, that is—just what you put into it. Remember, it is not the kitchen that makes the cook, but the cook that makes the kitchen!

Some very great restaurants and hotels do not have large kitchens. They are adequate, but not large. My own kitchen is six feet by nine feet. I have a large refrigerator but no separate freezer, and my work space is limited, yet I have been known to serve an elegant sit-down buffet dinner for forty people. How do I do it? Well, none of my space is wasted and I have pegboards all over the walls to hold the pots, pans, and utensils that I need. I have a three-tier utility table in one corner, on which I can put extra salads or vegetables that have been prepared and put aside until they are to be cooked. On many occasions, the dessert sits on the second shelf of the little table in the corner.

BASIC UTENSILS

I like good, solid, basic cooking pots and pans and a limited number of basic utensils, not a vast array of gadgetry. In France, I learned

3

to use my hands to mix together foods like salads, but a wooden spoon and fork will do! I do find, however, that an electric mixer, a blender, and a pressure cooker are indispensable "modern" aids to cooking that save hours of time.

Small utensils:
Automatic timer
Baster
Bottle opener (a good one)
Can opener
Cheese grater
Corkscrew
Food tongs
Garlic press
Jar opener (a good one)
Lemon press
Meat grinder
Meat thermometer
Paring knives
Pastry blender (hand-type)
Pastry brush
Pepper mill
Potato peeler
Potato scoop
Rolling pins (small and large)
Salt mill
Scissors (for cutting parsley, poultry, etc.)
Skewers
Slotted spoons (at least two)
Strainers (small, medium, and large)
Wire wisks (two sizes)
Wooden mixing spoons (various sizes, at least six)

Large utensils:
Board (large, for rolling pastry and for chopping)
Cake cover (large)
Cake racks (wire)
Carving knives (good ones)

Double boilers (two)
Food mill (shredder, chopper, grater)
Meat racks (wire)
Mixing bowls (graduated sizes)
Molds (various shapes and sizes, for bombes and mousses)
Pressure cooker (one should be enough)
Saucepans (assorted good, heavy ones; at least two large [8 quart], two medium [4 quart], and two small [1 or 2 quart] with lids)
Skillets (assorted good, heavy ones; at least two)

Electric utensils:
Blender
Ice crusher
Mixer

Miscellaneous:
Aluminum foil
Brown wrapping paper (small squares)
Paper towels
Rubber bands
String
Wax paper
Pencil

The list is not long or complicated, as you will see. Buy good, basic tools if you can afford them—in the long run they will save you time, energy, and money.

Special hint: Have handy on a shelf in your kitchen a small mirror, a breath sweetener, and a tiny spray cologne. It's nice to greet your guests without flour on your face, and kissing-sweet.

2 ৡ

Tips for Entertaining

BE CREATIVE IN YOUR COOKING

Often a simple, imaginative touch will do wonders for the most ordinary foods. Here are a few suggestions to start your imagination working:

Mix crisp bacon chips with buttered string beans or peas, or sprinkle them on top of an egg salad or a tomato or potato salad.

— Whip butter with your favorite herb in the blender and then chill to serve with steaks or roast beef, or on top of hot vegetables.

— Serve sour cream with chopped scallions or chives on baked potatoes—for added zest, put a tiny bit of anchovy paste in the sour cream.

— Serve your new potatoes with seasoned bread crumbs mixed with chopped parsley.

— Try potato chips with bits of grated cheese melted on them.

— Try a little peanut butter in a hot butterscotch or fudge sauce dessert.

— Sprinkle fresh coffee grounds on coffee ice cream.

— Use crushed corn flakes on apple pie or apple desserts.

— Add a few drops of almond extract to whipped cream for added flavor.

— Use honey and brown sugar on fresh grapefruit; pop under the broiler for a minute and serve hot.

— Use half mayonnaise and half whipped cream for fruit salads.

— Sprinkle grilled cheese sandwiches with cooked and drained, finely cut bacon just as the cheese begins to melt.

— Add some Burgundy wine to your old-fashioned beef stew.

— Add some seedless green grapes to your chicken salad.

— Pour a little sherry over some vanilla ice cream for an unusual dessert.

— For added zest in an oil and vinegar dressing, add some dry hot mustard powder.

— For those special luncheons, serve hot coffee with whipped cream on the side, plus crystallized sugar.

SHORTCUTS FOR COOKS

There are hundreds of shortcuts, of course; but I have found one or two that I use all the time, which I shall pass on here:

Skinning tomatoes: Drop the tomato into boiling water for just a second or two. You will find that it peels easily right away, or you can store it in the refrigerator until you want to skin it. The same is true of onions.

Hard-boiled eggs: Boil the eggs for exactly 10 minutes. Run the unshelled eggs under cold water until cooled. If they are not to be used immediately, store them in shells in the refrigerator. To shell eggs, crack all sides and peel under cold running water.

Cucumber moons: Scoop the seeds out of the cucumber and slice in half-moon shapes for a pretty effect.

Whirlpool method of poaching eggs: I found it the hardest thing in the world to make a perfect poached egg until I hit upon the whirlpool method. Drop the egg into salted water that is at the boiling point. Immediately take a kitchen tablespoon and circle the inside of the pot with it until the water is going in a circular motion. The egg will soon congeal; then it can be removed—perfectly cooked—with a slotted spoon.

GARNISHES

Garnishing food gives it that finished look. Garnishes are neither expensive nor time-consuming, but they are as important to food as that string of pearls or little gold pin is to a well-dressed look.

Garnishes also give you a chance to be creative. The other day I went to a party and the hostess put her *Eggs à la Russe* on a glass plate with daisies in-between and parsley on each egg. Imagination had transformed this simple appetizer into an elegant dish.

Radish roses: This simple garnish is easy to prepare. Cut the green leaves off the radish, but leave an inch or an inch and a half of stem. Wash in cold water and, holding the radish in one hand, start from the top and cut into strips, not going all the way down. Put your radish rose into ice water to open fully and for the stem to curl. It can be kept in cold water in the refrigerator for at least three days, but change the water each day.

Carrot and olive garnish: Serve sandwiches with this garnish. Take a thick carrot, peel it, and with a small, sharp knife, cut the carrot in a circular motion until you have a carrot snake. Make two snakes and place them on either side of the sandwich with olives in the little open rounds. If you make these ahead of time, keep them crisp in ice water.

Parsley: Parsley makes any dish look fresh and tasty. Sprigs of fresh parsley can be used to decorate any meat dish, or it can be chopped and sprinkled on top of vegetables. Fried parsley is delicious served with a hot entrée like veal parmigiana. Just drop the parsley, which has been washed and carefully dried with paper towels, into the hot fat for one-half minute. Take out and put on paper towels to absorb the grease.

Croutons or bread strips: Small croutons are best for soups, but a crouton about the size of a thumb with grated cheese on it, popped into the oven just before serving, is delicious with steaks and hamburgers.

Watercress: Watercress can be a difficult garnish, since it turns color and goes bad so quickly. When it is firm and crisp, however, I tie it in bunches with a bright green or gold ribbon and put four or five bunches around a crown roast of lamb. Hear the ooh's and aah's of your family and guests! Tied watercress bunches will also look very pretty next to any kind of roast or a chicken.

Pickles: Pickles, especially sweet gherkins, can make an appetizing and delicious decoration. Take the gherkin in one hand and slice down with a sharp paring knife almost to the bottom of the gherkin; then spread it to look like a fan. Four of these with a radish rose in the center look delicious on top of any salad.

Lemons: First carve out wedges from the outside of the lemon's skin. You can then cut the lemon in full-moon slices that have serrated edges. Or you can cut the lemon lengthwise in half first, which will give you half-moon slices. These will look very appetizing when used to decorate a fish fillet or a veal cutlet.

Mushrooms: Take care with mushrooms, since they will turn brown when they are peeled or cut. First cut off all but a quarter inch of the stem. Then peel and cut little wedges from the mushroom, holding it firmly in one hand by the remaining quarter inch of stem. This does take practice! Then drop the mushrooms into cold water, in which you have put lemon juice, until you are ready to take them out, dry them, and serve them. Or slice whole mushrooms very thin and spread them with a sharp cheese spread. Decorate fish or use as sandwich hors d'oeuvres. A cantaloupe or honeydew melon, cut flat in the shape of a pineapple ring, will make a pleasant change from pineapple on top of a ham steak. Some fresh seedless grapes sautéed in butter, placed in the middle of the melon slice hole, and decorated with parsley or watercress will transform your simple ham steak dinner into an elegant and delicious meal.

Cherry tomatoes: These are delicious dipped in batter and fried very quickly.

Chocolate curls: Take a chocolate bar (the six-ounce size) and run a paring knife along the side; form curls by slicing all the way down.

EDIBLE GARNISHES

	To Serve Hot	To Serve Cold
Bread	Small rounds or squares of thin-sliced bread can be sprinkled with cheese, bread crumbs, and parsley; dotted with butter; and put under the broiler. Serve around any hot egg or around tomato hors d'oeuvres.	Spread cream cheese on bread rounds or crackers. Sprinkle with chopped chives or scallions and serve.
Vegetables	Dip small cherry tomatoes in a batter made of a little flour, one egg, a little milk, seasoning, and some chopped parsley. Deep fry the batter tomatoes very quickly. Use to surround any plate of hors d'oeuvres. *Must be served hot!*	Slice a large mushroom into very thin slices. Spread a sharp cheese medium-thick on the mushroom slices. Decorate in a circle around any fish or sandwich-type of hors d'oeuvre. Radish roses, celery sticks, crescent moon cucumbers dipped in chopped parsley, tiny cubes of beet, can all be used to surround hors d'oeuvres.
Soup	Croutons (buttered bread cut into tiny squares and browned under broiler or baked until brown) are delicious in cream or bouillon soups. Croutons can also be dipped in soft cheese before browning (and before cutting up).	Cream cheese balls, very small and rolled in chopped parsley or chopped chives, are delicious in cold soups. Thin slices of tomato or sweet onion also taste very good.
Meat and Poultry	Deep-fry onion rings and cover with velouté sauce containing a pinch of mustard. Stuff mushrooms with sautéed and seasoned bread crumbs or with foie gras.	Make flowers of watercress or parsley, radish or turnip roses, carrot curls, fluted mushrooms, or stuffed hard-boiled eggs.

	To Serve Hot	*To Serve Cold*
	Sauté fruits (apple, orange, melon or pineapple) for poultry, pork and ham. Fry parsley.	
Fish	Sauté grapes and almonds for grilled fish. Hard-boil eggs; then cut them in half and stuff them with sautéed or seasoned bread crumbs or caviar. Fry parsley.	Serve lemon wedges with one surface dipped in chopped parsley, olives and pickles of all kinds, or sprigs of parsley or watercress.
Desserts	Cut white bread into narrow strips and brown under the broiler. (Spread with a heavy mixture of butter, cinnamon, and sugar before broiling.) This is especially good with soufflés or bombes.	Serve candied flowers of all kinds or whipped cream piped into rosettes. Chocolate curls pressed into the sides of cold soufflés or ice cream molds are attractive. Crystallized fruits, especially grapes, are good on desserts. Spun sugar is pretty on ice cream.

A WORD ABOUT HORS D'OEUVRES

The hors d'oeuvres should always be considered an important part of the meal. All too often, the hostess is inclined to consider the hors d'oeuvres as a "filler" to keep the guests happy while they have drinks and she is unobtrusively in the kitchen getting the dinner ready. But the good hostess plans the hors d'oeuvres, or appetizers, as carefully as she plans the whole meal. If they are to be served to guests who will be standing up, make sure that they are not runny, are easy to handle, and will not fall apart when picked up. If the guests will be served the appetizers while they are sitting down at the table, make the portions small and take care they are not overwhelming in taste. They should merely tease the taste buds and begin the flirtation with the appetite.

PARTIES WITH AND WITHOUT HELP

I will confess right away that if I have more than eight people to dinner, I hire a woman who comes in to serve and wash up afterward. I enjoy cooking, but I like to know that there is someone to serve the meal graciously and clean up later.

I go to many parties, however, where the hostess manages on her own very successfully. How much you spend on help will depend on your own budget and the importance of the occasion.

If you can afford help, take time to explain to them exactly what you want them to do. Explain your kitchen and your way of doing things. If everything is made clear beforehand, a quick trip to the kitchen to remind that it is time for cheese or that the ashtrays need emptying will be all that is needed.

If you don't have help, try to rinse dishes between each course. If you can get one load in the dishwasher, it's all to the good. It's also a good idea to have dessert and coffee in another room, so that you can leave the debris of the dining room behind.

TIPS ON BEING A GOOD HOSTESS

I have my menus and place cards ready before the guests arrive, of course, but I don't put them in place until I have seen how the guests mingle on arrival. In that way, I can place people who seem to be getting on well beside each other; I can avoid sitting a short person beside a very tall one; if one is left-handed, I can put him on the corner of the table; if one is very heavy, I can be sure he is not given a card-table chair. Another good tip to remember is to write the person's name on *both* sides of the place card—then the person across the table from him, as well as the people beside him, will know his name.

If the meal is a long one and the guests are at small tables for four or six, have the women change their tables just before dessert.

I always try to remember if any of my guests have food allergies or religious beliefs about certain foods, or just plain dislike something. I help my memory by keeping a little list of likes and dislikes next to the names of people I have entertained before. It is very flattering to be able to say to a guest, "I was going to serve broccoli since it is in season, but I remembered you didn't like it." Isn't that going to make your guests feel that time, thought, and care has gone into the meal?

In the same way, I try never to serve the same dinner to the same guests. If you keep a list of guests and next to it a copy of the menu served, you will easily be able to check on whether they have been given the same dish before.

As you give parties you find that some foods are more popular. It's a good idea to make a list of appetizers, salads, vegetables, cheeses and fruits, desserts, and beverages that went particularly well. Combining your most successful dishes will ensure an attractive menu.

Above all, keep your sense of humor. It will be infectious. Everything can be helped—from a collapsed soufflé to an electrical failure. If you keep your cool, your guests will sense your mood and enjoy your party—whatever happens.

ENTERTAINING PROGRESS CALENDAR

Everyone has a personal way of working out a timetable for a party. I offer mine as a guideline only—if it seems complicated to you, remember that it works for me because I have gotten into the habit of planning every detail well in advance so I can really enjoy the party.

Four weeks or more before:
Start making a guest list.
Decide on what kind of party it is to be.
Write out invitations or make phone calls.
Hire extra help, if needed.

Two weeks before:
Plan the menu.
Send reminder notes to those you only called.
Order rental equipment: extra chairs, tables, linens, etc.
Plan flowers and a tentative seating arrangement.

One week before:

Buy additional or unusual serving or cooking equipment, if needed.

Check your linen supply; buy needed extras and do any necessary laundry.

Shop for canned goods and other staples.

Check liquor, wine, mixer, and soft drink supplies.

Make a list of groceries, check the butcher to see if what you want will be in.

Order flowers.

Four days before:

Check any invited guests not heard from.

Polish silverware and brass; wash dishes and glasses if they have not been used for some time.

Make a tentative seating arrangement.

Write out individual menus and place cards.

Three days before:

Clean the house or apartment.

Order extra ice.

Two days before:

Start checking on everything to make sure you do not have to do it the next day.

This is a good day to buy things like extra cream, potatoes, and things that will not spoil.

One day before:

Have your hair done and get a manicure.

Check your dress to make sure it's all right; do the same for your husband's suit. Chose something elegant and appropriate, yet comfortable.

If you are having greens in big vases, get the greens from the florist and arrange them.

Set up and start arrangements on small tables, if you do not have small children.

Prepare any aspics or ice cream desserts.

Wash lettuce, spinach, and other vegetables that you can.

Have car washed if it's going to be in view outside.

Day of party:

Have flowers delivered early and set up.

Start preparing the necessary foods.

Make sure ice is delivered.

Put out clean ashtrays, matches, and cigarettes.

Lock up pets, if you expect to have guests that don't like them.

Freshen the bathroom by cleaning the mirrors and putting out guest towels.

Be sure that the closets to be used for guests' coats have enough room and hangers, or set up a party coat rack.

Feed young children early, and if young enough, get them into bed.

Take a shower, or, if possible, a leisurely bath. If you're organized enough to take time for a bath, my hat is off to you!

Be sure magazines and newspapers are in order.

Part I
Sit-Down
Dinners

3 ❧
Simple
Dinners

Simple Dinners: Menu I

APPETIZER:	Hot Shrimp Bisque
	(Can be done a day ahead)
MAIN DISH:	Chicken in Tarragon Cream
	(Can be done a day ahead)
SALAD:	Tomato and Cucumber Salad
	(Should be done the same day)
DESSERT:	Apple Pie
	(Can be done a day ahead)

HOT SHRIMP BISQUE
(Can be done a day ahead)   SERVES 8

Fish stock:
To make Hot Shrimp Bisque, you need fish stock made from

fish bones. Ask your fish man to give you some extra skin and fish bones.

> *1 pound fish bones*
> *¼ cup dry white wine*
> *6 pints water*
> *Salt and pepper*
> *1 carrot sliced in chunks*
> *1 small onion*
> *1 bay leaf*

To make the stock, put the fish bones in a large heavy pot with the dry white wine, water, salt and pepper, carrot, onion, and bay leaf.

Bring to a boil and then simmer for about 1½ hours. Strain.

Bisque:
> *1 pound raw shrimp*
> *Fish stock*
> *6 tablespoons butter*
> *4 tablespoons flour*
> *2 tablespoons tomato paste*
> *½ cup light cream*
> *Bread croutons for serving*
> *1 tablespoon chopped parsley or chives for serving*

While the fish stock is cooking, place the shrimp in about 2 pints water and cook until pink in color. Remove shrimp from water immediately. Cool slightly. Shell and devein. Wrap in foil and put into refrigerator.

Stop here if you are working ahead.

When preparing to serve, remove any fat from the top of the fish stock and put the stock into a large pot to warm. Reserve a few whole shrimp and put remainder into a blender. Add the blended shrimp to the stock. In another pot, melt the butter, stir in the flour, and slowly add the now warmed fish stock. Mix in the tomato paste, cream, and seasoning if needed. Heat very slowly. Do not allow to boil.

How to serve:

Cut the remaining whole shrimp into small pieces; when you put a ladle of soup into a cup or bowl, make sure that you include a piece or two of shrimp. Garnish with bread croutons and a little chopped parsley or chives.

This bisque can also be made with lobster. Substitute 1 pound of cooked lobster meat for the shrimp.

CHICKEN IN TARRAGON CREAM

(Can be done a day ahead)   SERVES 8

2 three-pound chickens
1 teaspoon salt
1 teaspoon pepper
2 tablespoons white wine
6 tablespoons chopped fresh tarragon
3 carrots, peeled and cut into large slices
2 stalks celery, cut up
2 tablespoons chopped parsley
2 large onions, cut in half

Make the stock from the necks, gizzards, and livers of the chickens. Put aside. Rub the chickens inside and out with the salt, pepper, white wine, and tarragon. Put the chickens in a large pot; cover with water; and add the carrots, celery, parsley, and onions. Cook slowly for 1½ hours. Do not overcook. Remove chickens from the pot, and when they are cool enough to handle, remove the skin carefully. Put the chickens back into the pot to cool. Then refrigerate the chickens in the stock.

Stop here if you are working ahead.

When preparing to serve, take the chickens out of the refrigerator and remove the fat from the top of the stock. Put the chickens and stock on top of the stove to warm while you make the cream sauce.

Cream sauce:
1 stick butter (¼ pound)
4 tablespoons flour
4 tablespoons white wine
1 cup chicken stock (from gizzards, necks, etc.)
1 cup medium cream
2 beaten egg yolks

Melt the butter in a skillet and stir in the flour. When it is a smooth paste, add the white wine and chicken stock. Stir until it thickens. Remove from heat and add first the cream and then the beaten egg yolks. Return to low heat and stir constantly until the sauce is thick, smooth, and creamy.

How to serve:
1 pound rice
Fresh tarragon

Boil rice while you are making the cream sauce.

Remove the chickens from the stock in which they have been warming. Place them on a bed of rice on a large serving platter. Pour the cream sauce over the birds so that it clings to them. Sprinkle a little fresh tarragon on top. You can cut the birds at the table or in the kitchen, whichever is easier for you, but show your guests the dish before you cut up the chickens. Serve extra sauce on the side.

TOMATO AND CUCUMBER SALAD

(Should be done the same day)   SERVES 8

1 head lettuce
4 medium-sized, skinned tomatoes
2 peeled cucumbers
Salt
Freshly ground pepper

Skin the tomatoes (see page 7) and slice thin. Cut the cucumbers slanted into medium-thick slices.

Put a leaf of the lettuce on a plate and arrange your tomatoes, and then the cucumbers. Season the salad with salt and pepper.

APPLE PIE
(Can be done a day ahead)   SERVES 8

Pie crust:
This recipe makes enough for a bottom and top crust. It is a good crust for quiche and meat pies as well as for fruit pies.

2 cups flour
4 egg yolks
4 tablespoons shortening
4 tablespoons sugar
1 teaspoon salt
1 beaten whole egg

Put the flour on a marble slab or pastry board. Make a well in the center and put in the egg yolks, shortening, sugar, and salt. Work center ingredients to a smooth paste; work flour in quickly. Make into a ball and wrap with wax paper. Put into the refrigerator for several hours; overnight is preferred.

Stop here if you are working ahead.

When ready to roll out, preheat oven to 350°, flour the board a little, and roll out the dough to a thin thickness. Take your pie pan, turn it upside down, and put the dough on it. Make the edges fluted, if you want to, or just trim it off neatly. Brush the beaten whole egg over the dough. Prick a few air holes and bake until it is nice and brown and crusty.

(If you are going to fill the pie before baking, be sure to put the crust into the pie pan, not on the back!)

Apple filling:
6 to 7 large, skinned apples
2 teaspoons lemon juice
Grated rind of lemon
2 tablespoons butter

1 tablespoon sugar
2 tablespoons peach or apricot jam
1 tablespoon cinnamon
1 teaspoon powdered sugar
Cheddar cheese or whipped cream for serving

Core the apples and cut them into thick slices. Put the sliced apples, lemon juice, grated rind of lemon, butter, and sugar into a large pan. Half cook the apples, cool a little, and add the apricot or peach jam. Fill the baked pie shell and sprinkle the top with cinnamon and powdered sugar. Put the top crust over the apples and prick it with a fork to allow some air holes. Brush the crust with a beaten egg, sprinkle on a little sugar, and be sure to seal the edges. Refrigerate.

Stop here if you are working ahead.

When you are ready to bake the pie, preheat the oven to 375° and bake for about 35 minutes or until golden brown. Remove and cool slightly. Serve warm.

How to serve:
Even something as simple as an apple pie can be made elaborate. Serving it warm with wedges of Cheddar cheese or with whipped cream is always nice. A friend of mine served her apple pie with a ceramic blackbird in the middle. It was a great hit.

Simple Dinners: Menu II

APPETIZER:	Cold Cucumber Mint Soup
	(Can be done a day ahead)
MAIN DISH:	Duck Supreme
	(Can be done a day ahead)
VEGETABLE:	Red Cabbage with Apples and Raisins
	(Can be done a day ahead)
DESSERT:	Lemon Meringue Pie
	(Can be done a day ahead)

COLD CUCUMBER MINT SOUP

(Can be done a day ahead)   SERVES 8

2 tablespoons butter
1 tablespoon olive oil
4 skinned cucumbers
1 medium-sized sliced onion
3 tablespoons flour
½ teaspoon garlic powder
1 cup chicken stock
1 cup light cream or half-and-half
1 cucumber with skin on
Chopped fresh mint

Melt the butter and oil in a large deep skillet. Add the skinned cucumbers and onion and fry gently. Add the flour, garlic powder, and then the chicken stock. Keep stirring until the mixture almost comes to the boil and thickens. The cucumbers should be mushy. Remove from the heat and put through a strainer. Put to the side and allow to cool. Refrigerate.

Stop here if you are working ahead.

When ready to serve, take the mixture from the refrigerator and add the light cream. Stir until it is completely blended. Test the soup seasoning before returning it to the refrigerator to chill.

How to serve:
Pour the chilled soup into a large glass bowl. Slice the unskinned cucumber very thinly, and keep the slices on a separate plate. Add one or two slices to each individual cup or bowl of soup, and sprinkle a little chopped mint on top of the cucumber slices. Be sure to keep this soup in the refrigerator until the last minute—it must be served cold to be really enjoyed.

DUCK SUPREME
(Can be done a day ahead)   SERVES 8

Duck is not too difficult to prepare, and yet I find it less and less wherever I go. This is sad because it is a delicious dish when cooked correctly. Try the following recipe the next time you want to impress someone.

2 five-pound ducks
4 tablespoons butter
2 teaspoons salt
2 medium-sized sliced onions
1 small crushed garlic clove
1 tablespoon sugar
10 peppercorns
4 strips bacon
¼ cup white wine
1 cup water
1–2 large oranges for serving
2 clusters of parsley or watercress for serving

Preheat the oven to 350°. Put the necks, giblets, and hearts into a saucepan of water to make stock. Tie some string around the ducks' wings and thighs to keep them in place. Slightly grease a roasting pan and put the ducks in it. Sprinkle the salt on the ducks, and place the sliced onions, the crushed garlic clove, sugar, and the peppercorns around the ducks. Put the bacon on top of the ducks. Pour in the wine and water. Roast uncovered until almost done, turning the ducks now and then. Save a little of the gravy drippings from the pan. Remove the ducks, wrap in foil, cool, and refrigerate.

Stop here if you are working ahead.

When preparing to serve, cut the ducks up into serving pieces. Warm the pieces by wrapping them again in foil, putting them into a pan, and heating them in a slow oven. Now make the gravy.

Gravy:
2 tablespoons butter
2 tablespoons flour
1 cup broth or duck stock (from necks, giblets, and hearts)
1 tablespoon gravy drippings
1 cup sliced mushrooms
1 teaspoon Worcestershire sauce
½ cup medium dry dark sherry

Melt the butter in a skillet; add the flour and blend. Add the broth, gravy drippings, the mushrooms, the Worcestershire sauce, and the sherry. Simmer very slowly, stirring all the time until thick. If the color is not right, add a little more sherry. The sauce should be thick and dark in color and delicious.

How to serve:
Take one or two large oranges, peel them in a spiral fashion with a paring knife, and place the curls of peel around the ducks. Slice the peeled oranges and place them around the ducks too. It's also nice to put a cluster of parsley or watercress at each end of the serving dish. Serve the gravy separately.

RED CABBAGE WITH APPLES AND RAISINS
(Can be done a day ahead)   SERVES 8

This red cabbage dish is delicious with duck, roast pork, or any kind of game.

1 large head red cabbage
½ cup wine vinegar
4 strips bacon or piece of salt pork
2 teaspoons sugar
½ cup water
3 peeled and quartered apples
¼ cup raisins
2 teaspoons salt
1 tablespoon red currant jelly

Cut the red cabbage into quarters. Slice thinly and place it in a heavy pot with the wine vinegar, bacon, sugar, and water. Allow it to come to a boil but watch carefully. If more liquid is needed, add water. Now add the apples, raisins, salt, and jelly. Cover and cook on low flame for about 2 hours. Take a look every so often and taste to see what else is needed. When finished it should be juicy but not soupy. Put into a big bowl, cool, and refrigerate.

Stop here if you are working ahead.

When ready to serve, warm again slowly. Do not allow to boil.

How to serve:
I like to serve the cabbage in a big white dish which sets off its elegant redness and richness.

LEMON MERINGUE PIE
(Can be done a day ahead)   SERVES 8

This short pastry recipe makes a good pie crust for Lemon Meringue Pie.

Pie crust:
2 cups flour
4 egg yolks
4 tablespoons sugar
2 tablespoons lard
2 tablespoons butter

3 *tablespoons ice water*
1 *teaspoon salt*
3 *tablespoons uncooked rice*

Put the flour on a pastry slab or your worktable. Make a well in the middle. Then add the egg yolks, sugar, lard, butter, ice water, and salt. Mix the center ingredients into a smooth but thick paste and quickly work into the flour. Make into a ball, wrap in wax paper, and refrigerate.

Stop here if you are working ahead.

When you are ready to roll out the dough, preheat the oven to 375° and roll out the dough, thinly, on a lightly floured board. Place the flan ring or pie tin on the cookie sheet, and carefully put the dough on the ring or pie tin. Take a piece of wax paper and put it in the middle of the crust. Put the uncooked rice on the wax paper. (The rice will keep the crust down while baking.) Bake for about 35 minutes until golden brown. Remove the paper and rice. Cool.

Lemon curd:
2 *grated lemon rinds*
Juice 2 lemons
1 *stick butter (¼ pound)*
1 *cup sugar*
3 *beaten eggs*

In the top of a double boiler, put the grated lemon rinds, lemon juice, butter, sugar, and beaten eggs. Stir constantly until the mixture thickens and coats the back of the spoon. When cool, fill the pie.

Meringue topping:
4 *egg whites*
6 *tablespoons sugar*

Beat the egg whites until stiff. When they hold a peak, carefully fold in the sugar. Pipe meringue from a pastry bag or a rose tube onto lemon filling, or you can just spoon the meringue on top of the pie. Sprinkle with a little granulated sugar and put into a low oven until golden brown.

How to serve:

Lemon Meringue Pie is pretty to look at just as it is, but I add a sprinkle of freshly grated lemon rind on top to give it a fresh lemon taste. Also, try putting some fresh white daisies on the serving dish around the pie—it's very attractive.

Simple Dinners: Menu III

APPETIZER: Eggs à la Russe
              (Can be done a day ahead)
MAIN DISH: Chicken Fricassee with Bread Crumb Dumplings
              (Can be done a day ahead)
SALAD: Lettuce and Tomato Salad
              (Should be done the same day)
DESSERT: Orange Mousse
              (Can be done a day ahead)

EGGS À LA RUSSE

(Can be done a day ahead)   SERVES 8

> *8 hard-boiled eggs*
> *3 tablespoons mayonnaise*
> *1 teaspoon peppor*
> *2 teaspoons salt*
> *1 teaspoon paprika*
> *1 tablespoon melted butter*
> *1 teaspoon hot mustard powder*
> *1 teaspoon lemon juice*
> *1 tablespoon chopped parsley*
> *Shredded lettuce or Bibb lettuce*
> *Gelatin coating (optional)*

Boil the eggs for 10 minutes. Put them under cold running water. When cool, refrigerate them in their shells.

Stop here if you are working ahead.

When you are preparing to serve, shell the eggs and cut them in half, trying not to break the whites. Remove the yolks and mash fine. Add mayonnaise, pepper, salt, paprika, melted butter, hot

31

mustard powder, and lemon juice to the mashed egg yolks. Pile this blend into the whites. Cover and place in the refrigerator.

How to serve:

Just before serving, shred the lettuce and put it on individual dishes or one large dish. Place the stuffed eggs on the shredded lettuce and put a little finely chopped parsley on each egg. You can also decorate the eggs with fancy toothpicks.

Special hints: If you are serving the Eggs à la Russe on individual plates, it is best to use Bibb lettuce leaves instead of shredded lettuce. You can add extra ingredients to the egg yolk mixture as you wish—a little chopped anchovy fillet, curry powder, chopped smoked salmon, pimientos, etc.

If it's a special occasion, you may want to give the eggs an elegant gelatin coating. Add 1 tablespoon plain gelatin to 1 tablespoon cold water, and dissolve in 2 tablespoons hot water. When the gelatin coating is clear, spoon a little over each stuffed egg half and put into refrigerator to set.

CHICKEN FRICASSEE WITH BREAD CRUMB DUMPLINGS

(Can be done a day ahead)   SERVES 8

Of the many chicken recipes I have, this one is my favorite. It's different, and it's very delicious.

2 three-pound fryers cut up
1 tablespoon salt
1 stick butter (¼ pound)
½ cup chicken stock
½ bar sweet butter
1½ cups bread crumbs
⅓ cup milk
2 whole eggs
1 teaspoon salt
1 tablespoon chopped parsley

Rub the skin of the chickens with salt. Melt the butter in a skillet; add the chicken pieces, skin down. Cook about 10 minutes on each side until the chicken is a yellowish color. Add a few ladles of chicken stock. Cover and then lower the heat. Simmer for about 45 minutes, or until tender. You can add more stock if you find it is cooking away, but not too much. Remove skillet from heat and put aside. When cool, put chicken and stock into dish, cover, and refrigerate. Now make the bread crumb dumplings.

Bread crumb dumplings:
Cream the sweet butter with a fork. Add the bread crumbs. Mix again with a fork. Add the milk and stir well together; then stir in the whole eggs, salt, and chopped parsley. Put to the side and let it harden slightly. Half fill a deep pot with cold water, salt, and some pepper and let it come to the boil. Make small dumplings from the bread crumb mixture by taking a spoonful of stuffing, rolling it into a ball, and dropping it into the boiling seasoned water. Do a few at a time; they will stay on the bottom of the pot to begin with, but as they cook, they will rise. Let them stay on the top for about a minute; then remove them and put them to the side. Finish all of them. Leave them in a small bowl, adding a very little of the chicken stock to keep them from sticking together and from drying out.

Stop here if you are working ahead.

When you are preparing to serve, make the following sauce for the chicken and bread crumb dumplings.

Sauce:
½ stick butter (⅛ pound)
3 tablespoons flour
½ cup chicken stock
3 tablespoons grated cheese
2 tablespoons sour cream

Melt the butter in a small saucepan. Remove from heat and stir in flour to make a smooth paste. Return to heat and add stock slowly. When sauce has thickened, add grated cheese and sour cream. Stir until thick and smooth. Taste for seasoning.

How to serve:

It's best to put this dish into a deep tureen. Put the pieces of chicken on the bottom and the rich sauce on the top. Then add the dumplings around the sides. They will blend into the sauce, but that's what you want. Add more sauce over them.

You need no other vegetables with this meal—only a large, fresh salad.

LETTUCE AND TOMATO SALAD
(Should be done the same day)   SERVES 8

This is a very refreshing salad, but you must use very good tomatoes.

1 head lettuce
4 medium-sized skinned tomatoes
Salt and pepper to taste

Make these salads on individual salad plates. Use nice big leaves of lettuce; then slice the skinned tomatoes very thinly. Sprinkle with salt and pepper and serve.

ORANGE MOUSSE
(Can be done a day ahead)   SERVES 8

1 envelope plain gelatin (1 tablespoon)
1 tablespoon cold water
1 cup fresh orange juice
1 tablespoon cornstarch
Grated peel of one orange
4 separated eggs
4 tablespoons fine sugar
½ cup heavy cream

In a small custard cup, soak the gelatin in the cold water. Heat the orange juice in a good-sized saucepan. Keep on the heat for only about a minute; do not boil. Remove from heat and slowly dissolve the gelatin in the orange juice; then add the cornstarch and the grated orange peel. Return to stove and heat very gently until the mixture thickens, stirring all the time. (This might take about 5 minutes, but do not leave the stove.) Cool. While this mixture is cooling, beat the egg yolks and the sugar together in a small bowl until light and yellow in color. Add the egg yolks and sugar mixture to the orange juice while it is still lukewarm. Put to the side. Beat the egg whites until they are stiff. In another bowl beat the heavy cream until it is stiff. Fold first the egg whites and then the cream into the now-cooled orange juice mixture. Pour into a ring mold that has been rinsed with cold water. Refrigerate for at least 5 hours, or better still, refrigerate overnight. Serve this mousse with orange sauce.

Orange sauce:
1 orange peel
1 sliced orange
2 tablespoons orange marmalade
1 teaspoon Grand Marnier liqueur
½ cup heavy cream

Cut the orange peel into tiny pieces. Take the orange slices and put them into a small pan with the orange marmalade and the Grand Marnier. Put in the little pieces of the orange peel, too. Heat until the marmalade is melted and the orange slices are soft. Remove from the heat and put to the side to cool. Whip the heavy cream and add it to the now-cold orange slice mixture. Put into a small dish and refrigerate.

Stop here if you are working ahead.

When you are preparing to serve, dip the mold into hot water for an instant. Then turn it out onto your serving dish. The orange sauce is kept in a separate bowl and spooned over servings of the mousse. Your guests will rave about the taste of this dessert.

How to serve:
I like to put the mousse on a glass plate and the orange sauce in a pretty bowl beside it. Use a big spoon for the mousse and another spoon for the sauce.

Special hints: It is always nice to decorate foods, especially if they are to be placed on a buffet table. For an orange mousse, I take an extra orange, cut the peeling in a spiral, and place it in the middle of the mold. If you use a regular soufflé dish, the orange peel spiral can be put on the middle of the mousse. Pipe extra whipped cream into the middle of the spiral to keep it in shape.

For a lemon mousse, you can substitute ½ cup of lemon juice for the orange juice and add some extra sugar to the heavy cream, since lemon is more tart than orange. Eliminate the orange and use two fresh lemons, and when ready to serve, cut the rind of one lemon into very fine strips and sprinkle around the sides of the dish.

Simple Dinners: Menu IV

APPETIZER: Marinated Herring with Chopped Parsley
(Can be done a day ahead)

MAIN DISH: Pot-au-Feu
(Can be done a day ahead)

SALAD: Spicy Cucumber Salad
(Can be done a day ahead)

DESSERT: Lemon Ice Cream in Lemon Boats
(Can be done a day ahead)

MARINATED HERRING WITH CHOPPED PARSLEY

(Can be done a day ahead)   SERVES 8

1 cup sour cream
3 marinated herrings, cut into bite-sized pieces
8 thin slices dark bread
1 tablespoon butter
1 large, thinly sliced, sweet red onion
1 tablespoon chopped parsley

Put the sour cream in a small bowl and add the marinated herrings. Mix with a fork until blended. Refrigerate.

Stop here if you are working ahead.

When you are preparing to serve, butter the dark bread. Mix the sour cream and herrings again.

How to serve:

It's best to put the herrings in the cream sauce on individual dishes. Put at least 2 thin slices of onion on top and sprinkle with parsley. Add the buttered dark bread on the side.

POT-AU-FEU
(Can be done a day ahead)   SERVES 8

This is an easy dish to prepare. It is a rich dish, both in taste and in actual cost, but it goes a long way and is worth every penny you spend on it.

2 tablespoons vegetable oil
4-pound stewing chicken
4 pounds chuck boneless beef
2 pounds beef bones
4 large whole onions studded with 2 whole cloves each
4 cut up carrots
2 celery stalks with leaves on
1 tablespoon parsley
3 small cloves garlic, split
1 large bay leaf
10 cracked peppercorns
8 cups beef broth or stock
4 cups water
Salt to taste
1 pound Polish sausage
12 whole carrots
18 small whole white onions
6 whole leeks

Heat the oil in a large cooking pot. Add the whole chicken and brown it all over, turning it frequently. Then remove it and keep it to the side. Discard leftover oil. Into a clean pot, put the boneless beef, beef bones, onions with cloves, cut up carrots, celery stalks, parsley, garlic, bay leaf, and peppercorns. Add the beef broth, water, and a little salt. Bring this slowly to a boil, remove scum that forms on top, and taste to see if it needs more salt. Reduce heat, cover, and simmer for an hour. Taste for salt, remove scum, and then add the browned chicken. Simmer, remove scum, and cook for two hours. Add the sausage, whole carrots, white onions, and leeks. Simmer for another hour. Keep skimming and test for tenderness of carrots and seasoning.

When the vegetables are tender, carefully remove the chicken, beef, sausage, whole carrots, white onions, and the leeks and arrange them on a deep serving platter. Strain the broth through a fine sieve into a large bowl or another deep oven-proof dish. Discard the leftover vegetables, herbs, and bones. Test the broth for seasoning. Pour a little of the broth onto the meat and vegetables to keep them moist. Cool. Cover with foil and refrigerate.

Stop here if you are working ahead.

When preparing to serve, reheat the broth first. When it is very hot, add the meat, and then when you are almost ready to serve, put in the vegetables.

How to serve:
This dish can be served in two ways. The meats and vegetables can be in a shallow dish, with chopped parsley sprinkled on top and the broth in a separate tureen; or the meat, vegetables, and broth can all be served from one tureen.

Have on hand Dijon mustard or horseradish, an assortment of sour pickles, and dark rye bread. I also have additional minced parsley in a small glass bowl in case anyone wants some.

Special hint: Try to save the marrow (the soft circle in the middle of the bones) from the beef bones. Put it aside, cut it into pieces and put it into the tureen just before serving. It's a delicious meal.

SPICY CUCUMBER SALAD

(Can be done a day ahead)   SERVES 8

> *5 small cucumbers*
> *1 teaspoon salt*
> *1 cup sour cream*
> *1 small clove crushed garlic*
> *1 teaspoon pepper*
> *1 teaspoon sugar*
> *2 tablespoons chopped fresh dill*
> *2 tablespoons tarragon vinegar*
> *¼ cup vegetable oil*
> *Bouquets of tarragon or dill*

Skin the cucumbers and cut them into very thin slices. Place on a flat dish and sprinkle with the salt. Cover with foil and put into the refrigerator for about 2 hours. Take them out of the refrigerator and squeeze out the water. Put them back into refrigerator.

Stop here if you are working ahead.

The day of the party, take a screw-top jar or a small bowl and put the sour cream, crushed garlic, pepper, sugar, fresh dill, tarragon vinegar, and oil in it. Mix until well blended and put aside until ready to use.

How to serve:
Besides being good to eat, this is a nice-looking salad. I like to serve it on a shallow glass dish. It's nice to place your cucumber slices in a line, sprinkle the dressing over them, and then put bouquets of tarragon or dill in the corners of the dish. You can also put the cucumbers into the bowl of dressing and mix with a fork until well blended.

LEMON ICE CREAM IN LEMON BOATS
(Can be done a day ahead)   SERVES 8

> 1 cup heavy cream
> ½ cup sugar
> 8 large lemons
> Juice and rind of 1 lemon
> Sprigs of mint or small pieces of chocolate round for serving

Whip together the heavy cream and sugar until very stiff. Place in the refrigerator.

Stop here if you are working ahead.

When you are preparing to serve, cut the lemons in half and remove the inside pulp. Cut a thin slice off the bottom of the lemons so that they will sit straight and steady on a plate. Take the whipped cream mixture out of the refrigerator and add the juice and rind of one lemon. Spoon it into the empty lemon halves. Refrigerate.

How to serve:
Put the lemon halves on glass or dark-colored plates to show off the yellow color. Put 2 halves on each plate with a sprig of mint on the top or a small piece of chocolate round. It's delicious.

4

Gourmet Dinners

The menus that follow are a little more complicated than those given in Chapter 3, "Simple Dinners," but by no means are they too complicated for the cook who plans ahead.

Gourmet Dinners: Menu I

APPETIZER: Cold Paradise Soup
(Can be done 2 days ahead)

MAIN DISH: Chicken with Grapes and Vegetables
(Can be done a day ahead)

SALAD: Spinach Salad
(Should be done the same day)

DESSERT: Chocolate Roll
(Can be done a day ahead)

COLD PARADISE SOUP

(Can be done 2 days ahead)   SERVES 8

To me, this is the best cold soup I can make. It is very refreshing and easy to prepare.

2½ pounds ripe tomatoes
3 teaspoons salt
1 teaspoon pepper
1 teaspoon seasoned salt
2 tablespoons vegetable oil
½ teaspoon onion juice
Grated rind of 1 lemon
1 cup tomato juice
3 tablespoons sour cream
1 medium-sized melon (cantaloupe or honeydew)
2 large cucumbers
2 tablespoons finely chopped parsley
8 medium-sized ice cubes

Skin tomatoes (see page 7) and put them through a sieve. You should have about 3 cups of tomato puree. Put the puree into glass bowl and add salt, pepper, seasoned salt, oil, onion juice, grated lemon rind, and tomato juice.

Stop here if you are working ahead.

When you are preparing to serve, the puree will be a little thick. Taste for seasoning and add the sour cream. If it is still too thick, add some more tomato juice to it; however, it should not be too thin, and the ice cubes will dilute it somewhat. Put back into refrigerator to keep cold. Cut the melon in half and use a potato scooper to make melon balls. Do the same with the cucumbers. Put the melon and cucumbers into separate bowls. Refrigerate. Chop the parsley very fine.

How to serve:

Pour the soup into glass bowls, only ¾ full. Put an ice cube in the middle, add two melon balls and two cucumber balls, sprinkle with the chopped parsley, and serve. It's delicious!

CHICKEN WITH GRAPES AND VEGETABLES
(Can be done a day ahead)   SERVES 8

Chicken should never be overcooked or it will lose its delicate flavor. If the chicken is tender and juicy, it is a very satisfying meal. If you are looking for that "best recipe," try this one.

1 stick butter (¼ pound)
2 tablespoons salt
2 tablespoons pepper
2 three-pound chickens
1 medium-sized bay leaf
1 small clove crushed garlic
½ cup water
¼ cup white wine

4 medium-sized carrots cut into fingers
1 medium-sized turnip cut into fingers
1 diced leek
1 small stalk diced celery
½ pound diced green beans

1 cup chicken stock
½ cup medium cream
1 teaspoon summer savory (or oregano)
1 teaspoon thyme
1 cup skinned white seedless grapes
Bouquets of parsley for serving

Preheat the oven to 350°. Rub a smàll piece of butter, salt, and pepper into the cavities of the chickens. Take the bay leaf and crushed garlic and also rub them into the cavities. Leave them inside. Spread butter with salt and pepper on the wings and tops of the chickens. Tie the wings and legs in place with a soft string. Place the chickens in a roasting pan with the water and wine. Roast in the preheated oven for at least 1 hour, turning the chickens and basting them every 15 minutes.

While the chickens are roasting, prepare the vegetables. Melt the remaining butter in a large skillet. Add the carrots, turnip, leek, celery, and green beans. Sauté until tender but not soft, 10–15 minutes. When the chickens are cooked, remove them from the oven and cool. Strain the gravy from the roasting pan and save it. Refrigerate vegetables, chickens, and gravy separately.

Stop here if you are working ahead.

Before reheating the chickens, let them stay at room temperature for about ½ hour and remove the bay leaf and crushed garlic from the cavities. Combine the gravy and stock and heat the mixture on top of the stove. Add the chickens to warm them. Do not allow to boil. Heat vegetables separately. When chickens are hot, remove and place them on a serving platter in a low oven. Strain the gravy and add the cream, summer savory, and thyme to it. Add the grapes just before serving.

How to serve:
For a buffet dinner, I cut up the chickens before putting them on the serving dish. For a sit-down dinner, I carve them at the table. Display this dish with the chickens in the center of the serving plate, the vegetables around the sides, and the gravy with grapes poured over the chickens. Decorate whole chickens with paper frills on the wing tips and bouquets of parsley on either side.

SPINACH SALAD

(Should be done the same day) SERVES 8

1 package fresh spinach
1 small, thinly sliced Bermuda onion
6 thinly sliced radishes
½ cup wine vinegar
½ cup water
¼ cup sugar
1 teaspoon salt
1 well-beaten egg
2 sliced hard-boiled eggs
1 can flat anchovies

Wash the spinach and dry it thoroughly with a towel. Break the spinach leaves into desired size (not too small) and put into salad bowl. Add the onion and radishes. Into a small saucepan, pour the vinegar, water, sugar, and salt. In a small bowl on the side, beat the egg with wire whisk or beater. Add the beaten egg to the vinegar mixture and bring to a boil. Let it cool, and just before you serve, sprinkle with dressing and toss. Garnish with the sliced hard-boiled eggs and anchovies.

How to serve:
I like to serve this from a wooden salad bowl onto individual glass salad plates.

CHOCOLATE ROLL
(Can be done a day ahead)   SERVES 8

How I love this dessert! If anyone asks me what dessert I love most, I always say with joy, "the Chocolate Roll." It's rich, but it's good.

> *8 ounces sweet milk chocolate*
> *3 tablespoons water*
> *1 teaspoon instant or already-brewed coffee*
> *6 large eggs*
> *1 cup fine sugar*
> *1 cup whipped heavy cream*
> *1 tablespoon almond extract*
> *4 tablespoons cocoa*
> *2 tablespoons raspberry jam*
> *Extra whipped cream*

Preheat the oven to 350°. Melt the chocolate with the water and coffee in the top of a double boiler over hot but not boiling water. Cool. Separate the eggs. Add the sugar to the egg yolks and beat until creamy and light yellow in color. Add the melted and cooled chocolate. Take a cookie pan or jelly roll pan and grease it; then take a piece of wax paper long enough to cover the entire pan with a little to fold over, and grease it also.

Beat the egg whites until stiff. Fold into egg yolk–chocolate mixture until well blended. Spread in pan and bake in preheated oven for 15 minutes. Then turn the oven off, but keep the mixture in the oven for another 5 minutes. Remove from the oven and cover with a dish towel that has been dunked in cold water and wrung out. Cool for 1 hour.

While the cake is cooling, whip together the heavy cream and the almond extract. Remove the cloth from the top of the cake. Loosen the cake from the wax paper and the bottom of the pan. Sprinkle some of the cocoa on top. Put extra wax paper on the table and sprinkle it with the remaining cocoa. Turn out the cake onto the wax paper. Peel the wax paper from bottom of cake. Spread the raspberry jam and then the whipped cream onto the cake. Roll it up like a jelly roll, using the wax paper to prevent the roll from breaking. Use wax paper to lift the roll onto a serving dish. Cut away the extra wax paper and refrigerate.

Stop here if you are working ahead.

An hour before your guests arrive, remove the cake from the refrigerator and sprinkle with confectioners' sugar, or leave it as it is.

How to serve:
I like to serve the Chocolate Roll with extra whipped cream in a small bowl next to it. Place fresh flowers on each side, or a pretty ribbon bow at the end, or just put it on paper doilies. Cut the roll on the slant.

Gourmet Dinners: Menu II

APPETIZER: Gruyere Cheese Teasers
(Can be done a day ahead)

MAIN DISH: Swiss Steak with Vegetables and Potato Balls
(Can be done a day ahead or the same morning)

SALAD: Romaine, Endive, Cucumber, and Watercress
(Must be done the same day)

DESSERT: Fresh Berry Bombe
(Can be done at least a week in advance)

GRUYERE CHEESE TEASERS
(Can be done a day ahead)   SERVES 8

½ pound Gruyere cheese, grated
1 package (2 ounces) cream cheese
1 tablespoon softened butter
2 tablespoons flour
1 tablespoon rice flour
¾ cup milk
1 teaspoon salt
1 teaspoon cayenne pepper
1 egg, beaten
½ cup bread crumbs
1½ cups oil

Into a pan put the grated cheese, cream cheese, butter, flour, rice flour, milk, salt, and cayenne pepper. Stir over the fire until thick. Put the mixture on a plate and let it cool. Refrigerate.

Stop here if you are working ahead.

When you remove the plate from the refrigerator, take a big spoonful of the cheese mixture and form into small balls; roll them in a little extra flour you have put on the side, brush with the beaten egg, roll in the bread crumbs, and fry in oil until golden brown. Place them on paper towels to absorb the excess grease. Serve immediately.

Helpful Hint: Sometimes your hands get very sticky working with melted cooled cheese, but if you can remember to put a little flour and a few bread crumbs on your fingers before you pick up a spoonful to make the Cheese Teaser, you will find it easier.

How to serve:
This dish is like a soufflé; it's best if your guests wait for it.

You can serve them all on a big wooden platter or on a pretty dish with lace doilies on it. Use fancy toothpick servers, or if you prefer, pass toothpicks around in a pretty wicker basket and let the guests help themselves.

SWISS STEAK WITH VEGETABLES AND POTATO BALLS

(Can be done a day ahead or the same morning)   SERVES 8

    4 medium-sized carrots
    1 pound string beans
    4 tablespoons vegetable oil
    8 six-ounce bottom round steaks
    2 tablespoons flour
    1 cup beef or chicken stock
    2 tablespoons tomato puree
    1 teaspoon salt
    1 teaspoon pepper

To save time, you can wash, trim, and cook the carrots and green beans the day before. Cut the carrots and the beans into 2-inch lengths. Boil each vegetable separately until tender but not soft: about 5 minutes or less for the beans, 10 minutes for the carrots. Heat the oil in a heavy skillet, and brown the meat on both sides quickly. Remove and put steaks to the side. Combine flour, stock, tomato puree, salt, and pepper. Heat and stir until thick. Refrigerate the steaks and save the gravy.

Stop here if you are working ahead.

Before you serve, heat the skillet. Put in the gravy and steaks, and heat together until hot. If the gravy needs more liquid or seasoning, add it now. Heat vegetables in separate pan. Season.

How to serve:
Serve this dish on a large copper pan with the steaks on the bottom, the gravy on the top, and the vegetables on top of the gravy and steaks.

I like to serve this dish with Potatoes Parisienne (see page 62), but no other vegetable is necessary if you are watching your waistline.

ROMAINE, ENDIVE, CUCUMBER, AND WATERCRESS SALAD
(Must be done the same day)   SERVES 8

2 cucumbers
Head romaine lettuce
Bunch watercress
3 medium-sized endive

Peel the cucumbers, cut them down the middle, remove the seeds with a spoon, and then turn them upside down and slice into thin, crescent-shaped slices. Wash and drain the romaine and watercress and absorb the excess moisture on a towel; break into pieces, put into a bowl, cover with a damp paper towel, and put into the refrigerator. The endive and the cucumbers should be put into a small bowl, covered, and refrigerated.

Stop here if you are working ahead.

When you are ready to serve this salad, remove the romaine, watercress, endive, and cucumbers from the refrigerator. Put them all into a wooden or glass bowl and prepare the salad dressing.

Dressing:
4 tablespoons olive oil
2 tablespoons vinegar

1 teaspoon salt
1 teaspoon pepper
1 teaspoon Dijon mustard
½ teaspoon sugar

Combine all ingredients in a screw-top jar. Shake until blended. Taste for added seasonings. Mix the salad together quickly after the dressing has been added and serve at once.

FRESH BERRY BOMBE

(Can be done at least a week in advance)   SERVES 8

1 pint vanilla ice cream
1 pint strawberry ice cream
1 pint fresh strawberries
½ teaspoon almond extract
1½ pints whipped heavy cream
Extra sugared strawberries for serving
Extra whipped cream for serving

Choose the mold you want, and then soften the ice creams together in one bowl. When soft, mix them together. Clean the fresh strawberries separately and add them to the softened ice cream. Mix the almond extract into 1 pint of the whipped heavy cream and stir into the ice cream mixture. Press the combined ice creams and cream mixture into the mold. Put into freezer.

Stop here if you are working ahead.

When you are preparing to serve the bombe, unmold it onto a glass dish. Decorate with the remaining ½ pint of heavy whipped cream.

How to serve:

Have a glass bowl with extra fresh sugared strawberries and one with whipped cream on the side, for those who do not care about calories.

Gourmet Dinners: Menu III

APPETIZER:	Hot Salmon Mousse *(Must be done the same day)*
SOUP:	Potage Cressonniére (Watercress and Potato Soup) *(Can be done a day ahead)*
MAIN DISH:	Le Coq au Vin Blanc (Chicken in White Wine) *(Can be done a day ahead)*
SALAD:	Mixed Greens with French Dressing *(Should be done the same day)*
DESSERT:	Rum Form Cake *(Can be done a day ahead)*

HOT SALMON MOUSSE

(Must be done the same day)   SERVES 8

If you want an unusual appetizer, try this one. It is very good and will set you up as a gourmet cook!

2 pounds cooked salmon
3 egg whites
1 teaspoon salt
1 teaspoon pepper
1 teaspoon cayenne pepper
1 pint whipped heavy cream
1 tablespoon chopped parsley
Velouté or Mousseline Sauce
Wedges of lemon for serving
Sprigs of parsley for serving

Preheat oven to 350°. Put the salmon in a blender and chop fine. Turn out into a large bowl. Beat egg whites in a separate bowl until very stiff. Fold the egg whites into the salmon mixture. Add the salt, pepper, and cayenne pepper. Now very carefully mix in the whipped heavy cream.

Lightly grease a mold of your choosing, add the mixture, cover with lightly greased wax paper and set into a shallow pan of hot water. Bake in 350° oven for about 30 minutes. Carefully unmold it and serve with Velouté Sauce or Sauce Mousseline (see page 190).

How to serve:

Put the Hot Salmon Mousse on a large, heat-proof platter. Decorate with lemon wedges and big sprigs of parsley. Serve the sauce in a sauce boat.

Slice the mousse on the slant. It's prettier that way and you can then put it down on a plate instead of having it fall, as it does when you cut it straight. Put sauce, a wedge of lemon, and a sprig of parsley on each slice.

POTAGE CRESSONNIÉRE (Watercress and Potato Soup)
(Can be done a day ahead) SERVES 8

This soup holds many wonderful memories for me. To pass my test and qualify for a Cooking Diploma from Dione Lucas, I had to make about five recipes in two hours and the Potato and Watercress Soup was one of them. It was difficult but I passed, and this was the way I made the soup.

5 tablespoons butter
2 large sliced onions
7 medium-sized quartered potatoes
1 small clove finely chopped garlic
2 cups water
Pinch salt and pepper
2 bunches washed watercress
3 cups milk and half-and-half cream (1½ cups each)

Melt the butter in a large, deep pot. Slightly brown the onions. Now add the potatoes, garlic, and water. Cook very slowly until potatoes get mushy. Rub through a coarse strainer. Add salt and pepper. Put into a bowl and place in refrigerator when cooled.

Stop here if you are working ahead.

When you are preparing to serve, return potatoes to the deep pot and warm. Add the watercress, milk, and half-and-half cream. Taste again for seasoning. Heat, but do not allow to boil. Simmer and serve.

How to serve:
Just put a flower of watercress into every cup or bowl. Nothing else is necessary.

LE COQ AU VIN BLANC
(Can be done a day ahead)   SERVES 8

2 chickens, each cut into 8 pieces
2 tablespoons flour
1 teaspoon salt
1 teaspoon pepper
4 slices bacon, cut into small pieces
1 small clove crushed garlic
16 small onions, peeled but kept whole
½ pound mushrooms, cut in half
1 cup white wine
3 cups chicken stock or water
Bouquet garni
1 teaspoon salt
1 teaspoon pepper

Roll the chicken pieces in the flour, salt, and pepper. While you are doing this, cook the bacon pieces in a large skillet until they are lightly browned. Add the garlic, and when it is cooked and browned, remove both the bacon and the garlic. Add the chicken pieces and brown on both sides. Remove the chicken but keep it warm. Now add the onions and mushrooms and sauté them.

Take a deep pot and put into it the wine, stock or water, the bouquet garni—parsley, thyme, bay leaf and chervil tied up in a square of cheesecloth—and the salt, pepper, chicken pieces, bacon, garlic, onion, and mushrooms. Cook under moderate heat for 1 hour.

Remove the bouquet garni and taste for seasoning. Cool and put everything into a large bowl. Refrigerate.

Stop here if you are working ahead.

When preparing to serve, remove the layer of fat from the top of the cooled stock. Put into a pot and heat slowly. Do not boil. Taste for seasoning.

How to serve:
Bring Le Coq au Vin Blanc in, covered, in a deep casserole. When you have it on the table, remove the cover and allow the wonderful aroma to travel throughout the room. Be sure you put a little bit of everything on each plate—onion, mushroom, a little bacon, and at least two pieces of chicken. Hot French bread is a must with this dish. It also can be served with rice.

MIXED GREENS WITH FRENCH DRESSING
(Should be done the same day) SERVES 8
The simplicity of this salad is what makes it so good.

1 head Bibb lettuce
Handful iceberg lettuce
Handful fresh spinach
French dressing (see page 192)
Salt
Pepper

Wash and dry the lettuce and spinach. Dry thoroughly with paper towels. Break the lettuce and spinach into a salad bowl. Use French dressing and a little salt and pepper. Toss, taste, and serve.

RUM FORM CAKE
(Can be done a day ahead) SERVES 8
Rum Form Cake is delicate and very delicious. Try it for your next dinner party.

¾ cup vegetable shortening
2 cups sugar
3½ cups sifted cake flour
5 teaspoons baking powder
1 teaspoon salt
1½ cup milk at room temperature
1 teaspoon vanilla extract
½ teaspoon almond extract
6 egg whites

Preheat oven to 350°. Grease and lightly flour 3 eight-inch layer cake pans. The cake can also be made in a single eight-inch springform cake pan.

Cream the shortening, add the sugar gradually, and beat with beater for about 2 minutes to really blend them together. Take a wooden spoon and slowly add the flour, baking powder, and salt, blending alternately with the milk, all together. Add the vanilla and almond extract. The mixture should be well blended. In another bowl, beat the egg whites until they hold peaks. Carefully fold them into the mixture. Pour into the greased pans and bake for about 35 minutes in 350° oven. While the cake is baking, make the filling. When baked, take cake out of oven and let cool.

Rum form cake filling:

6 egg yolks
1 cup sugar
½ teaspoon salt
⅓ cup chopped walnuts
1 cup white raisins soaked in rum
½ cup rum

Beat the egg yolks and add the sugar, salt, chopped walnuts, and raisins. Put all this in the top of a double boiler and stir constantly. When it is good and hot, add the rum. Cook until the mixture becomes thick. Remove from the heat and cool. Put aside.

Stop here if you are working ahead.

When you are preparing to serve the cake, trim if necessary to make even layers. Put the filling in between. If you use a springform pan, cut the cake into three even layers, spread with the filling, and put the layers together. Sprinkle powdered sugar on top of the cake or cover it with the following icing.

Rum form cake icing:

2 egg whites
5 tablespoons cold water
1½ cups sugar
½ teaspoon cream of tartar

Put all the ingredients into the top of a double boiler. Mix thoroughly. When they are blended, use your beater and beat until the mixture starts to form peaks. Be patient. This may take as long as 8 to 10 minutes. When peaks begin to form, remove from heat and continue beating until icing is perfect for spreading. Cool.

How to serve:

After icing this cake, I like to put a handful of chopped walnuts on the top or around the sides. A little bowl of heavy cream whipped with a little rum in it is an extra plus for this already delicious cake.

5 ❧
Elegant Gourmet Dinners

In this chapter, we progress one step further to larger and more complicated menus, but they are still well within the reach of the dedicated cook.

You will note that one entry is common to all three menus—the *Intermezzo*. The Intermezzo is a must when you are having an elegant dinner and a lengthy one. It is good for the palate and it is good for conversation.

I first discovered the Intermezzo at a restaurant in Manhattan. It pleased me so much that it is a ritual I always perform at our elegant dinners at home.

The Intermezzo is simply a small amount of lemon or lime sherbet (other flavors are too sweet) served in a liqueur glass immediately before the entrée. The tart, tangy taste acts to neutralize the taste buds before the main course.

Elegant Gourmet Dinners: Menu I

APPETIZER:	Fresh Caviar on Toast Points with Vodka *(Must be done the same day)*
SOUP:	Hot Consommé Unique *(Must be done the same day)*
SALAD:	Bibb Lettuce Salad with Watercress and Cucumbers *(Must be done the same day)*
INTERMEZZO:	Lime Sherbet
ENTRÉE:	Baby Pheasants Stuffed with Wild Rice *(Can be done a day ahead)* Potatoes Parisienne *(Can be done a day ahead)* Puree of Spinach *(Can be done a day ahead)*
CHEESE AND FRUITS	*(Can be done a day ahead)*
DESSERT:	Ice Cream with Sherbet Mold *(Must be done 1 or 2 days ahead)* Baby Cream Puff with Coffee Whipped Cream Filling *(Can be done a day ahead)*

FRESH CAVIAR ON TOAST POINTS WITH VODKA

(Must be done the same day)   SERVES 8

4 hard-boiled eggs
1 teaspoon salt
3 tablespoons chopped parsley
4 medium-sized finely chopped onions
8 slices buttered white toast

Cut the eggs in half and carefully remove the yolks. Finely chop both yolks and whites separately. Add a little salt to the yolks. Put the chopped egg whites, chopped egg yolks, chopped parsley, and chopped onions into separate small bowls. Toast the bread, butter it, and cut it in half diagonally.

How to serve:
Put the caviar on a mound of ice, in a glass bowl or in the jar you purchased it in. Put the garnishes around the caviar and serve the buttered toast on a separate dish. Have spoons for each garnish. Vodka served in small jigger glasses with the caviar is a big success and very delicious.

HOT CONSOMMÉ UNIQUE
(Must be done the same day) SERVES 8

This is a very simple soup, but by dressing it up a little, you can serve it at your most elegant party.

6 cups chicken stock
2 cups clam broth
Salt and pepper to taste
½ pint whipped heavy cream
1 tablespoon chopped parsley

Put the chicken stock and the clam broth into a large pot. When it starts to get hot, test for seasoning. Add salt and pepper if necessary. Whip the heavy cream until it is good and thick.

How to serve:
Make sure your cups or bowl are warmed. Add a ladle full of the broth and put a full tablespoon of whipped cream on top. Add a sprinkle of parsley and serve.

BIBB LETTUCE SALAD WITH WATERCRESS AND CUCUMBERS

(Must be done the same day) SERVES 8

  2 heads Bibb lettuce
  1 bunch watercress
  2 large cucumbers
  Salt and pepper to taste

Wash and thoroughly dry the lettuce and watercress. Tear into pieces. Skin and cut the cucumbers into thin slices. Put everything into a large salad bowl. Add the salt and pepper. Toss in a vinegar and oil dressing, such as Sauce Vinaigrette (see page 194). Serve at once.

INTERMEZZO

Serve a liqueur glass of lime sherbet to each guest.

BABY PHEASANTS STUFFED WITH WILD RICE

(Can be done a day ahead) SERVES 8

  8 small pheasants, 1½ pounds each (one for each guest)
  1 pound cooked wild rice
  2 whole beaten eggs
  ¼ cup white raisins
  Dash nutmeg
  1 large cut up black truffle
  2 tablespoons red wine

Preheat oven to 375°. Make sure the pheasants are clean, inside and out.

Put the cooked, drained wild rice into a large bowl. Add the beaten eggs, white raisins, nutmeg, cut up pieces of truffle, and red wine. Mix well. Scoop enough to fill the cavity of each pheasant. Tie the legs and the wings of the pheasants with soft string. Butter the birds and cover them with foil. Put them into a preheated oven and cook for 1 hour. Take out and let cool. Refrigerate.

Stop here if you are working ahead.

When you are preparing to serve, heat the oven to 375°, put the pheasants in without the foil paper, and cook an additional 30–45 minutes. Baste the birds and get them well-browned.

Gravy:
Butter or fat
Flour
Pan drippings
1 cup chicken stock

While the pheasants are browning, make the gravy by combining some butter or fat, flour, some drippings from the pan, and at least 1 cup of chicken stock. Cook until the gravy thickens.

How to serve:
Take the birds out of the oven and remove the strings while keeping the gravy hot and thick. Taste gravy to see if it needs any salt or pepper.

Then put all the pheasants on a large silver platter. Decorate by putting lamb frills on the drumsticks and placing watercress sprigs all around the tray.

POTATOES PARISIENNE
(Can be done a day ahead)   SERVES 8

   10 large peeled potatoes
   2 cups water
   1 teaspoon salt
   ½ cup vegetable oil

After you have peeled the potatoes, make potato balls of them with a scooper. Allow about 4 balls for each person. Put them into salted water and cook until almost soft. Drain off the water. Put the vegetable oil into a skillet and add the potato balls. Allow the potato balls to finish cooking and begin to brown. Salt a little more. Wrap in foil and refrigerate.

Stop here if you are working ahead.

When preparing to serve, unwrap the foil, put some chips of butter into the skillet and brown the potato balls until they are crispy and delicious.

How to serve:

Put the Potatoes Parisienne around the pheasants in clusters. They will look much better that way. If you have 8 people over for dinner, do them in clusters of 4. Potatoes Parisienne are always a big hit.

PUREE OF SPINACH

(Can be done a day ahead)   SERVES 8

> *5 pounds fresh spinach (washed and cleaned)*
> *½ cup water*
> *1 teaspoon salt*
> *1 cup heavy cream*
> *1 stick butter (¼ pound)*
> *½ teaspoon ground nutmeg*
> *Lemon slices for serving*

After the spinach has been washed and cleaned, put it into a large pot with the half cup of water and salt. Cover and cook very quickly—only a minute or two. When the spinach is cooked, remove it from the heat, drain it, and put it into a bowl. Cool and refrigerate.

Stop here if you are working ahead.

When you are preparing to serve, put the cooked spinach into a blender, adding cream a little at a time to keep the blender working smoothly. When done, put to the side. Melt the butter in a large skillet and add the blended spinach. Add the rest of the cream, test for seasoning, and add the ground nutmeg. Be sure you do not cook the puree too quickly. Serve.

How to serve:

The best way to serve this excellent vegetable is by putting it into a large pretty white dish and decorating it with slices of lemon.

CHEESE AND FRUITS
(Can be done a day ahead)

You can serve as many varieties of cheese as you want, but if you want to keep to just three different kinds, try French Brie, Port Salut and a Black Diamond Cheddar or a tangy Roquefort. A good selection of crackers and breads is important.

As for the fruits, I serve only grapes in the winter time, but in the summer I have small pears, apples, apricots or plums, and cherries. I never have oranges, big apples, or peaches. I find they are difficult to eat and sometimes overpower the excitement of the wonderful cheeses. The fruits should be washed, ripe, and ready to eat. Always have either grape scissors or small cutting knives near by.

BABY CREAM PUFFS WITH
COFFEE WHIPPED CREAM FILLING
(Can be done a day ahead)   SERVES 8

1 stick butter (¼ pound)
1½ cups water
2 cups flour
1 teaspoon salt
6 eggs

1 cup heavy cream
½ cup sugar
2 tablespoons of already brewed strong coffee

Heat butter and water in a large saucepan. Just before it begins to boil, add the flour and salt all at once and stir quickly and vigorously. The mixture will turn to paste and come away from the pan, almost forming a ball. It should take about 5 minutes. Remove from the heat and cool a little. When cool, add the eggs, one at a time. Beat after each egg is added. The dough will then be even and shiny and have a well-blended texture.

Preheat oven to 450°. Lightly grease a cookie sheet; then divide the dough according to the size of puff you want, but keep them small for this recipe. Remember they will spread, so don't put them close together. Bake for about 25 minutes, when they will be puffed up. Turn off the oven and open the oven door. Let the puffs cool before removing them from the oven. Cover with foil and refrigerate.

Stop here if you are working ahead.

Just before serving, split the puffs and remove some of the inside. Take ½ pint of heavy cream and whip it until it's very stiff. Then whip in the sugar and the strong coffee. Scoop the mixture into the individual Baby Cream Puffs. Serve.

How to serve:

Put doilies on a large glass or silver tray. Put the cream puffs on it, sprinkle them with powdered sugar, and see how quickly they will be off the table into a very satisfied guest.

ICE CREAM WITH SHERBET MOLD
(Must be done 1 or 2 days ahead)   SERVES 8

The contrast between the smoothness of vanilla ice cream and the tartness of the lemon or lime sherbet gives this dessert special interest.

2 pints vanilla ice cream
1 pint lemon or lime sherbet
Slices of lemon or lime for serving
Sprigs of fresh mint for serving

Put the vanilla ice cream into a bowl and soften it. Get the mold you want and run some cold water over it. Take most of the softened ice cream and press it down into the mold. Then take the sherbet and put it into the middle. Finish off with the ice cream and put into the freezer.

Stop here if you are working ahead.

When preparing to serve, remove the mold from the freezer and turn out (put it into a little hot water for a second or two) onto a pretty glass or copper dish. If the hot water has melted the outside of the ice cream, put the dish and ice cream mold into freezer for about 5 minutes.

How to serve:

Decorate with a circle of thin slices of lemon or lime and sprigs of fresh mint. When you cut into the mold, notice the colors and the different textures.

Elegant Gourmet Dinners: Menu II

APPETIZER:	Soufflé Lobster Supreme
	(Can be done a day ahead)
SALAD:	Belgian Endive with French Dressing
	(Can be done a day ahead)
INTERMEZZO:	Lemon Sherbet
ENTREÉ:	Filet of Beef with Truffle Sauce
	(Can be done a day ahead)
VEGETABLES:	Artichoke Bottoms with Pureed Peas
	(Can be done a day ahead)
	Potatoes Anna
	(Must be done the same day)
ASSORTED	
CHEESE	
WITH GRAPES	*(Can be done a day ahead)*
DESSERT:	Fruit Tart with Paper-Thin Crust
	(Can be done a day ahead)

SOUFFLÉ LOBSTER SUPREME
(Can be done a day ahead)   SERVES 8

This is a time-consuming appetizer, but the results are worth all the effort and time taken to produce it.

½ cooked lobster
3½ tablespoons butter
1 finely cut medium-sized carrot
1 finely cut medium-sized onion
1 tablespoon chopped chives
1 tablespoon chopped parsley
½ cup vegetable oil

1 teaspoon paprika
2 tablespoons Cognac
½ cup dry white wine
1 cup heavy cream
3 tablespoons dry sherry
Slices of lemon or lime for serving
Sprigs of parsley for serving

Cut up the cooked lobster into chunky pieces and put to one side. In a large skillet, melt 2 tablespoons of butter and put in the chopped carrot and onion. Cook very slowly over low heat until soft, not brown. Add the chopped chives and parsley and remove from heat. Heat the oil in a large shallow pan. Add the lobster and the vegetables, and then sprinkle on the paprika. Mix together and add the Cognac, white wine, and heavy cream; cook for about 15 minutes over a low heat. Remove the lobster from the pan, cool, and refrigerate. Keep cooking the remaining liquid until it reduces itself to half. Add the sherry and 1½ tablespoons butter. Put the sauce aside to cool. Add the lobster. Refrigerate.

Batter:
2 tablespoons butter
¼ cup flour
¾ cup hot milk
½ teaspoon salt
6 separated eggs
¾ cup grated Parmesan cheese
½ teaspoon cayenne pepper

Melt the butter in a saucepan. Add the flour and cook until it almost turns light brown. Then add the hot milk and the salt. Stir until the mixture gets thick. Put it aside to cool and refrigerate.

Stop here if you are working ahead.

Preheat the oven to 375°. When preparing to serve, put the lobster mixture into the greased soufflé mold. Let the batter mixture come to room temperature. Then add the beaten egg yolks. Whip the egg whites until they are very stiff and fold them in. Mix in the cheese and cayenne pepper. Add the batter on top of the lobster mixture and put it into the oven. The batter will rise and absorb the juices. The cooking time is 30 minutes.

How to serve:

Let your guests wait for the soufflé, then bring it to the table so everyone can see it. Have the sauce in a separate dish and a big spoon nearby so that you can scoop out the soufflé. Garnish with a slice of lemon or lime and a sprig of parsley. This is a super dish.

BELGIAN ENDIVE WITH FRENCH DRESSING

(Can be done a day ahead)   SERVES 8

   1 pound medium-size endives
   1 teaspoon celery seeds
   1 teaspoon ground pepper
   ½ cup French dressing (see page 192)
   Dry mustard (optional)

Separate the leaves of the endive. Do not cut them because cut leaves must be eaten immediately or they will turn brown, and they look more attractive if just separated. Make sure they are cold.

How to serve:

Place the endive on a large glass plate or a wooden tray in a sunburst fashion. Sprinkle the celery seeds and then the ground pepper over the endive. Pour the French dressing on evenly but carefully. Make sure you have a large spoon and fork with which to serve the endive.

Special hint: I find that when I sprinkle a little dry mustard on the endive after I put the celery seeds around, it gives the French dressing a sharper taste.

INTERMEZZO

Serve a liqueur glass of lemon sherbet to each guest.

FILET OF BEEF WITH TRUFFLE SAUCE

(Can be done a day ahead)   SERVES 8

> *5–7 pound filet of beef*
> *2 chopped shallots*
> *2 tablespoons butter*
> *¼ cup claret*
> *½ cup stock*
> *2 tablespoons extra-fine flour*
> *Truffles*

The filet of beef is a pyramidal piece of beef, weighing 5–7 pounds, cut from the loin of the steer, near the kidney. It is an elegant piece of meat. It can be browned in a heavy pan, or roasted or cooked over direct heat, but it must be served rare, never overdone. If you are doing it in the oven, preheat to 450°.

While the meat is cooking, lightly sauté the chopped shallots in the butter. Add some claret, and let the liquid reduce itself by half over the heat. Add the stock and quickly stir in 2 tablespoons of extra-fine flour to thicken. Do not cook your meat all the way through (only about half an hour for a 7-pound roast). Put aside to cool, wrap in foil, and refrigerate. Save the stock gravy and the truffles.

Stop here if you are working ahead.

Let the meat sit at room temperature for about 1 hour before you finish the cooking. Then, in a 400° oven, cook the meat quickly (5 to 7 minutes per pound) so that it is still rare. In a separate small pot, add some of the truffles to the sauce and heat gently.

How to serve:

Put the filet on a large platter. Cut it into 1-inch slices, pour the sauce over it, and sprinkle with the remaining truffles.

ARTICHOKE BOTTOMS WITH PUREED PEAS

(Can be done a day ahead)   SERVES 8

> *8 fresh green artichokes*
> *2 cups water*

1 teaspoon salt
2 teaspoons lemon juice
2 packages frozen peas
1 tablespoon fat
2 tablespoons flour
Salt and pepper to taste
4 tablespoons cream
Butter for serving
Grated cheese for serving

Cut off the artichoke leaves, trimming off until you get to the bottoms. Be sure to remove all the "choke." Then cook the bottoms in the water with salt and lemon juice added. (You can also buy canned artichoke bottoms.) When the leaves are soft, remove them from the water and let them cool. Trim them more if needed; then put them on a large sheet of foil and keep to the side. Cook and drain the peas. Rub through strainer. Melt the fat in a pan. Add the flour and a little salt and pepper. Brown slowly and then add the pureed peas. Cook a few minutes and then add the cream. Scoop out and add to the artichoke bottoms. Wrap in the foil and refrigerate.

Stop here if you are working ahead.

When preparing to serve, take the artichoke bottoms from the refrigerator and keep them at room temperature for about an hour. When your meat dish is ready to be cut, heat the filled artichoke bottoms in the 350° oven and, just before serving the filet of beef, put them under the broiler and let them brown slightly.

Special hint: When you put the filled artichoke bottoms under the broiler, it's best to put some chips of butter and some grated cheese on them. This is a great dish.

POTATOES ANNA
(Must be done the same day)   SERVES 8

8 medium-sized potatoes, peeled and sliced almost paper thin
1 stick butter (¼ pound)

2 teaspoons salt
½ cup medium cream
Parsley for serving
Thinly sliced carrots for serving (optional)

Grease a round mold or baking dish with a little butter; line the mold following a pattern of thinly sliced potatoes, butter, salt, a little cream, potatoes, butter, salt, and so on until it is all finished. Preheat the oven to 400°. Bake in the oven for a good hour until tender.

How to serve:
The best way to serve this dish is to invert the mold and garnish it with parsley. Slice the mold like you would a pie. This is delicious.

Special hint: You can also add thinly sliced carrots; they add color, rather than change the taste.

ASSORTED CHEESE WITH GRAPES
(Can be done a day ahead)

Please see my suggestions on page 64

FRUIT TART WITH PAPER-THIN CRUST
(Can be done a day ahead)   SERVES 8

Paper-thin pie crust:
1 stick butter (¼ pound)
1 cup flour
1 teaspoon sugar
1 egg

Work the butter into the flour, cutting with two knives or a pastry blender—mixture should look like cornmeal. Sprinkle on the sugar and add the egg; then work the sugar and egg into the mixture with a fork. Make into a ball, wrap in wax paper, and put into the refrigerator for 3 hours or more. When ready to roll out, preheat the oven to 400° and get out a 9-inch pie pan. Roll out the dough very thinly, fit it on the pie pan, prick it in several places, and put it in a 400° oven for 15 minutes. When baked, remove, cool, and keep for next day.

Stop here if you are working ahead.

Filling:
Fresh or canned fruit
Powdered sugar
Ground plain cookies
Whipped cream
Crushed walnuts (optional)

Pick your fruit according to the season. If you use fresh fruits (such as pitted cherries, peaches, blueberries, or strawberries), be sure to sprinkle them generously with sugar before using. If you use canned fruits (such as Bing cherries, apples, or peaches), be sure you drain them. Sprinkle some ground plain cookies on the crust before you add the fruit so it is not soggy.

Keep the pie crust at room temperature for about 15 minutes. Then add the fruits, sprinkle a little powdered sugar on them, and decorate with whipped cream.

How to serve:
The canned fruits are usually presweetened so an unsweetened whipped cream is best, but on a fresh fruit tart I have found that you need to sweeten the whipped cream. Never completely cover the fruit with the cream; make sure enough fruit shows. Sometimes it's nice also to crush some walnuts and sprinkle on top of the whipped cream.

Elegant Gourmet Dinners: Menu III

APPETIZER:	La Petite Marmite *(Can be done 3 days ahead)*
INTERMEZZO:	Lemon or Lime Sherbet
ENTREÉ:	Rack of Spring Lamb *(Must be done the same day)*
VEGETABLE;	Potatoes Parisienne *(Can be done a day ahead)*
SALAD:	Caesar Salad with French Dressing *(Must be done the same day)*
DESSERT:	Black Walnut Fudge Pudding *(Can be done a day ahead)*

LA PETITE MARMITE
(Can be done 3 days ahead)   SERVES 8

This is an expensive soup because you use a lot of meat, but you can stretch it into at least two meals.

4 quarts cold water
Chicken legs, breast, wings, and neck
2 pounds beef flank or shoulder
4 soup bones with marrow
1 tablespoon salt
1 teaspoon pepper
4 medium-sized carrots cut into chunks
1 medium-sized quartered turnip
1 large onion with 2 cloves in it
1 small quartered onion
Bouquet garni
Grated Parmesan cheese for serving
Chopped parsley for serving
Toasted French bread for serving

Into a large heavy pot, put the water, chicken, and beef. Allow to come to a boil. Now add the soup bones. Simmer for 1 hour. Skim the white fat from the top. Add the salt, pepper, carrots, turnip, whole and quartered onions, and the bouquet garni (see page oo). When the mixture starts to reboil, skim the fat again. Allow it to simmer covered for 2 hours. Remove from heat and allow to cool. Separate meat and vegetables and put them into small bowls. Save the marrow and throw away the bouquet garni.

Stop here if you are working ahead.

When you are preparing to serve, remove any fat that has set on top of the stock. Cut the beef and chicken into strips. Cut the vegetables in the shapes you want—in strips or small chunks—but keep them uniform. Test the seasoning. Do not save the cloves. Break up the whole onion if it hasn't broken while cooking.

How to serve:
If you are serving this dish on a buffet table, put the chicken, beef, and the vegetables into a large tureen. Add the marrow. Around the soup tureen have small glass bowls in which you have grated Parmesan cheese, chopped parsley, and small round slices of toasted French bread.

INTERMEZZO

Serve a liqueur glass of lime sherbet to each guest.

RACK OF SPRING LAMB
(Must be done the same day)   SERVES 8

Not everyone enjoys lamb, but if you like lamb you will love Rack of Spring Lamb. Serve this only if you know the guests you are inviting will enjoy it.

1 rack spring lamb (both legs and part of loin left attached)
1 teaspoon Dijon mustard

1 teaspoon flour
1 teaspoon salt
1 teaspoon pepper
½ teaspoon marjoram
½ teaspoon mint
1 clove garlic (optional)
2 tablespoons flour
½ cup red wine
½ cup chicken or vegetable stock
½ teaspoon chicken gravy concentrate
Fresh watercress or mint for serving

Preheat the oven to 475°. Make sure the butcher has cut the carcass up the back and trimmed the legs, so that the rack will be easy to cut and handle once it is cooked.

Rub the lamb with the mustard, flour, salt, pepper, marjoram, mint, and if you like, a little bit of garlic. Set in the oven on a shallow pan for 30 minutes at 475°; then turn down the heat to 350° and cook until done.

Roasting time should be about 1½ hours because the lamb should be slightly pink on the inside, not well done. Baste at least every half hour. To make the gravy, spoon out into a saucepan some of the fat from the pan while the rack is roasting. Mix in the flour to a smooth paste. Add the wine and stock. Then add the gravy concentrate to darken a little. Taste and add seasoning as necessary. The gravy should not be thick. Keep warm.

How to serve:

The best way to serve this dish is to first show it to your guests whole on a big platter. You can put a lamb frill on each rib with a toothpick if you like. Surround it with fresh watercress, and place a bowl of mint jelly at the side. If you can get fresh mint in a bunch, use it instead of the watercress. It is not always easy to find. Carve the rack of lamb in the kitchen where you can grab a strong hold on it, or if you are skillful at carving, show it off by doing it at the table. Serve it with Potatoes Parisienne (see page 62).

CAESAR SALAD WITH FRENCH DRESSING

(Must be done the same day) SERVES 8

> 1 *large bunch romaine lettuce*
> 1 *small clove crushed garlic*
> 2 *slices white bread cut into crouton size (¼ inch cubes)*
> ½ *cup olive oil*
> 2 *teaspoons lemon juice*
> 1 *teaspoon salt*
> *Dash black pepper*
> *Small can flat fillet anchovies*
> 2 *well-beaten eggs*
> ¼ *cup grated Parmesan cheese*

Wash the romaine lettuce carefully and dry it with paper towels. Break each leaf into about 3 pieces and place them in a large salad bowl. Into a small skillet put the crushed clove of garlic, bread cubes, and 1 tablespoon of the oil. Sauté until the bread cubes are browned. Discard the garlic and drain. Keep the bread cubes warm. Make your French dressing by putting into a screw top jar the rest of the olive oil, lemon juice, salt, pepper, and a little of the oil from the can of anchovies; shake well. Add the well-beaten eggs to the salad bowl. Toss lightly, coating the leaves all the time. Add the Parmesan cheese and toss again. Add the well-shaken French dressing and put in the bread croutons and pieces of anchovies.

How to serve:

It is best to make a show out of serving Caesar Salad—you can make it at the table if you like. Bring in the romaine, washed and already in the salad bowl. At the table, add the eggs, French dressing, cheese, the bread croutons, and anchovies. Don't give your guests too much because it is a very rich salad. It's great!

BLACK WALNUT FUDGE PUDDING

(Can be done a day ahead) SERVES 8

> 1 *cup sifted flour*
> 2 *teaspoons baking powder*

½ teaspoon salt
½ cup sugar
3 ounces grated semi-sweet dark chocolate
1 cup coarsely chopped black walnuts
½ cup milk
1 teaspoon vanilla extract
2 tablespoons melted butter
¾ cup dark brown sugar
1¾ cups hot water
½ pint whipped heavy cream

Before you start, preheat the oven to 350°. Into a mixing bowl sift the flour, baking powder, salt, sugar, and 2 tablespoons of the grated chocolate. Mix in the nuts; then stir in the milk, vanilla extract, and melted butter. Grease an 8- or 9-inch square baking pan. Spread the batter in it.

Put the brown sugar, the rest of the grated chocolate, and the hot water into a small bowl. Pour this over the batter already in the pan. Do not mind the way it looks, because it will look odd, but it does turn out very well. Bake for about 20 minutes or until the center is set. Remove it from the oven, set it aside, and allow it to cool.

Stop here if you are working ahead.

Take the pudding out of the refrigerator about 2 hours before you serve it. Reheat it in the oven for about 15 minutes. You will find that it is a pudding floating on top of a delicious chocolate sauce. Cool only slightly before serving. Be sure to whip the heavy cream. Do not add any sweetener to it.

How to serve:
Serve this dish in a large glass bowl, or if you cooked it in a very attractive oven-proof dish, you can serve it in that with the whipped cream in a glass dish next to it, or you can just spoon the whipped cream on top. It is delicious and I promise that you will not have a bite left.

Part II
Informal
Entertaining

6 ﷽

How to Run a Buffet Party

Buffet parties are an ideal way to entertain a large number of people. But buffet entertaining should not mean that the food is not as delicious and thoughtfully prepared as it would be for a more formal, sit-down dinner. Since you will have more food to prepare, I have tried to include menus that can be prepared very largely ahead of time. As I cannot repeat too often—good planning is the secret of being a good hostess.

SETTING UP THE BUFFET TABLE

When you are planning the buffet table, remember that your guests will see it as a whole. You must, then, strive for balance and drama to make an effective display of the food to be served. Try to visualize how your menu will look on the buffet table in terms of shape and color, the dishes you will use to show it off, and how it will have to be grouped to be both attractive and practical.

Try for a dramatic centerpiece of flowers or crystal, or for a display at both ends—never use an unbalanced display. In the same way, try for a good balance of foods; I like to have at least two of every kind of dish—two appetizers, two meat dishes, two salads, two desserts. This will give your guests plenty of choice, and for those with food allergies or prejudices, there will be more than enough to eat.

Here are a few simple rules to follow in setting up your buffet table:

— Do not serve food that guests have to carve for themselves. Everything should be cut up in the kitchen beforehand and presented in serving-sized pieces.
— Be sure to keep hot food hot and cold food cold.
— Make your serving plates steady—nothing is worse at a buffet party than a serving dish that wobbles or slides.
— Don't overfill the serving dishes; always leave enough room for the serving spoon to be put in without the dish spilling over.

If you have enough room in your serving area around the main buffet table, set up two small sidetables. On one table you can place the plates, utensils, napkins, water glasses, condiments, etc. On the other table you can place the cups and saucers and tea and coffee. This arrangement keeps people moving and avoids congestion around the table.

THE PARTY WORKSHEET LIST

It's an excellent idea to clip a list of the menu to be served onto your refrigerator door when you are having a large buffet party. It's only too easy to forget that aspic mousse in the cellar refrigerator when you have a great deal to organize!

SETTING UP THE BUFFET BAR

At a buffet party, you will need to set up a bar if you don't have a regular bar in your house. This is true whether you have a barman for the evening or let your guests help themselves. The following is a guide to what you will need to have a well-stocked, efficient bar for a party:

Bar supplies:
Plenty of ice (crushed and cubed), ice bucket, tongs

Glasses (different sizes for different drinks)
Coasters
Stirrers
Straws
Can opener and bottle opener
Lemon squeezer and strainer
Sharp knife and cutting board
Long-handled bar spoon for stirring
Jiggers
Cocktail shaker
Bottle caps and corks
Paper towels
Cocktail napkins
Trays to serve on
Bartender's guide
Pad and pencil to take large orders
Corkscrew

How much will your guests drink? As a rough rule of thumb, you must allow 1 drink per guest per half hour. In a large group, it's a good idea to have small glasses; so often a guest will put down a half-empty glass and walk away from it. For this reason, you'll be wise to allow for 3 glasses per person.

Purchasing Guide for Drinks:

Type of beverage	Size of bottle	Number of drinks per bottle
Champagne	1 fifth	7 to 8 drinks
Table wine	1 fifth	8 drinks
Dessert wine	1 fifth	10 drinks
Rum	1 fifth	16 drinks with 1½ ounce jigger
Gin	1 fifth	16 drinks with 1½ ounce jigger
Whiskey	1 fifth	16 drinks with 1½ ounce jigger
Vodka	1 fifth	16 drinks with 1½ ounce jigger
Sherry	1 fifth	10 to 12 drinks

The well-stocked liquor cabinet: This is what I consider necessary to have on hand for a well-stocked cabinet:

Liquor	Bourbon, rye, scotch, gin, vodka, rum
Soft drinks and mixes	Ginger ale, cola drinks, diet colas
Mixes	Soda water, quinine water, grape juice, tomato juice, orange juice
Fruits	Lemons, limes, cherries, olives, onions
Wines	Red, white, sherry, Dubonnet, sweet and dry vermouths
Liqueurs	Brandy, Drambuie, crème de menthe, Cognac

7 🦆
Fork–Only
Buffet Dinners

Fork–Only Buffet Dinners: Menu I

APPETIZERS:	Sardines au Gratin
	(Can be done a day ahead)
	Steak Tartare
	(Must be done the same day)
MAIN DISHES:	Breast of Veal Farcie
	(Can be done a day ahead)
	Beef Ragout with Onions
	(Can be done a day ahead)
	Chicken in Herb Cream
	(Can be done a day ahead)
SALADS:	Green Bean Salad
	(Can be done a day ahead)
	The Everything Salad
	(Must be done the same day)
CHEESE	
AND FRUITS	*(Can be done a day ahead)*
DESSERTS:	Berry Cheese Pie
	(Can be done a day ahead)
	Cinnamon Cake
	(Can be done a day ahead)

SARDINES AU GRATIN

(Can be done a day ahead) SERVES 8

4 medium-sized, peeled and thinly sliced potatoes
2 medium-sized, yellow, thinly sliced onions
2 tablespoons butter
20 small sardines
1¼ cups heavy cream
4 tablespoons grated Parmesan cheese
Lemon slices for serving

Preheat the oven to 400°. While the oven is heating, peel and slice the potatoes and onions. Butter a casserole dish. Place the potatoes on the bottom and the onions on top of them. Dot with butter all over. Place sardines on top of the onions. Cover and bake for ½ hour. Add the cream and bake for another 15 minutes. Take it out to cool. Refrigerate.

Stop here if you are working ahead.

About 2 hours before you serve this dish, take it out of the refrigerator and keep it at room temperature. Sprinkle Parmesan cheese over the top and put it under the broiler, allowing it to get hot and browned.

How to serve:
Serve this dish any way you want to, in a long skillet pan or in a shallow white dish. Just be sure it is hot and has small lemon slices around it.

STEAK TARTARE

(Must be done the same day) SERVES 8

This is a most wonderful appetizer. There are a few basic requirements to the recipe. You can elaborate on it as you like.

2 egg yolks
1½ pounds ground raw lean steak
½ cup chopped onions or scallions

1 tablespoon salt
1 tablespoon freshly ground pepper
1 tablespoon capers
½ cup chopped onions or scallions for serving
½ cup chopped parsley
Buttered dark bread, melba toast, or French bread for serving

Mix the yolks into the meat, adding the chopped onions or scallions. Add the salt, pepper, and capers.

How to serve:
Make a mound of meat with additional scallions alongside it. A small bowl of capers and chopped parsley can be put nearby. On another dish or plate, have buttered dark bread or melba toast. Some people even like slices of French bread. Have a variety. This is an excellent fork-only appetizer.

BREAST OF VEAL FARCIE

(Can be done a day ahead)   SERVES 8

When you are preparing veal it is good to remember that veal is a delicate meat and somewhat bland in taste.

2 five-pound breasts of veal
¼ cup white wine
2 cups stale bread cut into small pieces
1 cup milk or stock
3 whole eggs
1 tablespoon salt
1 tablespoon pepper
1 small chopped onion
1 tablespoon chopped parsley
1 cup cooked spinach
Butter
Bacon strips
2 dozen small white onions
8 medium-sized quartered potatoes

1 cup sour cream
Chopped parsley for serving

When you are ready to cook the veal breasts, spread them out and sprinkle them with a little bit of white wine. In a bowl put the bread, milk or stock, eggs, salt, pepper, chopped onion, parsley, and cooked spinach. With your hand or with a large fork, mix and blend; then mix and blend again. On each breast of flattened veal, put half of the stuffing and flatten it out. Roll them up tightly and tie with string. Rub some butter on them and fasten some strips of bacon onto the outside with toothpicks to keep them moist. Put into a large deep pot and cook at medium heat. Keep turning them while they cook to keep them moist; cook about ½ hour. Now preheat your oven to 375°. Put the small white onions and the quartered potatoes into the pot, sprinkle on a little more salt, and put the covered pot into the oven for about 1 hour. Baste from time to time. Do not cook completely. Take from the oven, cool, and refrigerate in the same pot.

Stop here if you are working ahead.

When preparing to serve, preheat your oven to 375° and put the pot with the veal and the vegetables into the hot oven. If any fat has settled on top, remove most of it before heating. Keep pot in the oven for 1 hour, basting frequently.

Remove veal from the oven and untie the strings. Take about 1 cup of the *gravy* and very carefully add the sour cream to it, stirring all the time. When the entire cup of sour cream has been added, put the mixture into the pot with the other gravy and stir until it is entirely mixed in.

How to serve:

Cut the veal breasts on the slant and put them in the center of an attractive platter with potaoes and onions on the side. Pour the gravy over the meat. Have some chopped parsley in a small bowl to sprinkle on top. If you are serving on a buffet table, this is an excellent fork dish because the meat is very tender. Have some gravy in reserve in a small gravy boat in case your guests want to add more.

BEEF RAGOUT WITH ONIONS

(Can be done a day ahead)   SERVES 8

When anyone mentions beef stew, it is usually accepted as a everyday dish; but if you prepare it properly and serve it with a flair, you can make it a most acceptable party dish. Let me show you how!

1 stick butter (¼ pound)
3 pounds top round beef cut into 2-inch squares
3 tablespoons hot sherry
24 small white onions
16 medium-sized mushrooms
2 teaspoons tomato paste
1 teaspoon meat glaze
4 tablespoons flour
1½ cups stock
1 cup red wine
1 teaspoon salt
1 teaspoon pepper
Bouquet garni
2 tablespoons chopped fresh parsley or dill

In a large skillet, melt the butter and when it is very hot, add the squares of beef, browning them quickly. Pour the hot sherry over them. Remove the beef from the skillet. Add the onions, brown them slightly, and remove them. Then add the mushrooms and sauté them about 2 minutes. Remove. The onions and mushrooms should be put aside. Put the tomato paste, meat glaze, and flour into the skillet and stir until well blended. Pour in the stock and stir very carefully until the gravy becomes smooth and thick, almost to the boiling point. Add the red wine, salt, pepper, bouquet garni (see page 54), and cubes of browned beef. (The cooked mushrooms and onions should not be added yet.) Cook the beef very slowly for at least 2 hours. Do not cover, but watch carefully and keep heat very low. If the sauce looks a little pale, add a little red wine to give it a browner color. When done, take off heat and put aside.

Stop here if you are working ahead.

When preparing to serve, remove the bouquet garni and add the onions and mushrooms. Check the seasoning again, and simmer until it is good and hot and ready to be served.

How to serve:
Serve in your prettiest casserole dish, and remove the cover when guests are coming to the buffet so that they can smell the aroma. Then sprinkle chopped parsley or dill over the meat. Serve with hot buttered rolls or French bread, and rice on the side if you want.

CHICKEN IN HERB CREAM
(Can be done a day ahead)   SERVES 8

This is a very special dish. The taste is superb even though it looks a little bland unless you dress it up as suggested below.

3 two and one-half-pound chickens
Pinch salt and pepper
3 tablespoons tarragon
4 carrots cut up into chunks
2 stalks celery cut up
1 tablespoon chopped parsley
4 small onions cut up
Water to cover chickens

After you have cleaned the chickens inside and out, rub the cavity and the outside with the salt, pepper, and tarragon. Put the chickens into a large pot with the carrots, celery, parsley, onions, and enough water to cover.

Bring to a boil and then simmer for about 1 hour. Do not allow them to overcook; the chickens must be tender, but they should not fall apart. Take the chickens out of the pot and remove the skin. Cut chickens into serving-sized pieces. Let them stand in their own juice, well covered with foil. Cool and refrigerate.

Stop here if you are working ahead.

When preparing to serve, skim any fat from the top of the

stock and put the chickens back into the pot with the stock. Heat gently while you cook the carrot fingers and make the sauce.

Sauce:
4 tablespoons butter
4 tablespoons flour
3 tablespoons fresh tarragon (or 2 tablespoons dried tarragon)
2 tablespoons fresh chopped parsley
2 tablespoons fresh thyme (or 1 tablespoon dried thyme)
½ cup white wine
2 cups chicken broth or stock
4 beaten egg yolks
1 cup heavy cream
1 pound cooked carrots cut into finger lengths

Melt the butter in a skillet, and then blend in the flour. Add the tarragon, parsley, thyme, wine, and chicken broth or stock. Remove from the heat and mix in the beaten egg yolks and cream. Stir until the mixture is smooth and thick. Take the chicken pieces, put them in the serving dish, and cover them with the herb sauce. Since there will be a lot of sauce, make sure the dish is deep.

How to serve:
If you are able to get fresh tarragon, sprinkle extra leaves on top after you have poured the sauce into the dish. Place the cooked carrot sticks in the dish in clusters. Delicious!

GREEN BEAN SALAD
(Can be done a day ahead)   SERVES 8

2 pounds green beans cut in half lengthwise
2 cups salted water
2 large, thinly sliced Bermuda onions
4 tablespoons wine vinegar
½ cup vegetable oil
1 teaspoon salt
½ teaspoon pepper

2 heads lettuce
2 tablespoons freshly chopped dill

Wash and split the green beans. Cook in salted water until they are tender but still crisp. Drain. Allow to cool. While beans are cooling, slice the Bermuda onions. Into the bean bowl pour the wine vinegar, oil, salt, pepper. Put into the refrigerator to keep cold.

Stop here if you are working ahead.

About an hour before your guests arrive, wash the lettuce thoroughly. Dry and keep it in paper towels in refrigerator.

How to serve:
Arrange the lettuce leaves around the sides of a glass salad bowl. Put the beans and the onions in the center and then sprinkle the dressing on them. Put the chopped dill on top.

THE EVERYTHING SALAD
(Must be done the same day)   SERVES 8

4 sliced hard-boiled eggs
6 finely minced anchovy fillets
1 teaspoon dry hot mustard
Pinch salt
Pinch pepper
1 cup chopped celery
1 cup cooked artichoke bottoms
2 heads Boston lettuce torn into pieces
¼ cup olive oil
2 tablespoons tarragon vinegar
½ cup canned beets cut into strips or left in slices

How to serve:
Arrange the slices of hard-boiled eggs on the bottom of a large glass or wooden salad bowl. Sprinkle the minced anchovy fillets on top of the eggs. Do the same with the mustard, salt, and pepper. Add the chopped celery, the artichoke bottoms, and the Boston lettuce. Toss around with your hands or with a salad fork

and spoon. Into a screw-top jar pour the oil and vinegar and little salt and pepper. Taste. Add more seasoning if necessary. Shake the dressing and put it on the salad just before you serve it. Place the beets on top. Delicious!

CHEESE AND FRUITS

I feel that a menu like this demands cheese and fruits at this point. Please see pages 64 and 143 for suggestions about what kinds of cheese and fruits to serve.

BERRY CHEESE PIE

(Can be done a day ahead) SERVES 8

When I say "berry pie," it can mean any kind of berry, but I find that raspberry is a great favorite and a little unusual. This is a heavy dessert, but if served in small wedges, even after a full meal, it's very satisfying.

Crust:
2 cups flour
1½ teaspoons salt
½ cup shortening
¼ cup ice water

Put the flour, salt, and shortening into a bowl. Cut into it with a pastry blender or two knives. When it is almost the consistency of cornmeal, add the ice water. Mix with a fork and form the dough into a ball. Put it on wax paper and refrigerate. It can also be frozen.

Stop here if you are working ahead.

Soften the cream cheese used for filling (see below). When you are ready to use the crust, preheat the oven to 375°. Roll out the dough on a lightly floured board, make it into a circle, and fit it into your pie plate. Fold the edges and flute the sides with your thumb or finger. Put aside.

Filling:
1 pound softened cream cheese
½ cup sugar
2 eggs
1 cup sour cream
*2 boxes fresh raspberries or 2 packages frozen raspberries
    (thawed)*
2 tablespoons cornstarch
1 cup whipped heavy cream
1 teaspoon almond extract
2 tablespoons confectioners' sugar

Put the softened cream cheese, sugar, and eggs into a small bowl and beat until smooth. Pour this into the pie plate. Bake in 350° oven for about 45 minutes. Test for doneness with a knife or wooden toothpick. If it comes out clean, the pie is done. Remove the pie from the oven and allow it to cool at room temperature. Then spread sour cream on top. Refrigerate for at least 2 hours. While pie is in refrigerator, put raspberries into a small saucepan with the cornstarch. Heat until the mixture thickens and becomes translucent and shiny. Cool to room temperature and fold in the whipped heavy cream. Pour on top of the cold pie. Refrigerate again.

How to serve:
Even though this is a very rich dessert, I still whip up extra heavy cream with almond extract to make rosettes around and in the middle of the pie. On top of each rosette I put a raspberry. Sprinkle with confectioners' sugar for display. I bet you not one bite is left over.

CINNAMON CAKE
(Can be done a day ahead)   SERVES 8

2 sticks butter (½ pound)
1 cup sugar
2 whole eggs

2 cups pastry flour
1 teaspoon baking powder
1 cup milk
1 teaspoon almond extract

Preheat the oven to 400°. It's best to take the butter out early to let it soften. Cream the butter with the sugar. Stir in the eggs, one at a time, until they are completely blended. You can use a wire whisk, but it's best to use an electric mixer. Sift the pastry flour, measure, and resift twice with the baking powder. Add to the batter alternately with a cup of milk into which you have put the teaspoon of almond extract. Pour into a shallow pan and bake for about 30 minutes. When you see the cake beginning to set, and before the crust appears, make the icing.

Special icing:

1½ cups brown sugar
2 tablespoons butter
¼ cup water
1½ tablespoons cinnamon
Extra whipped heavy cream or powdered sugar for serving

Combine the brown sugar, butter, water, and cinnamon in a saucepan. Bring to a boil and cook until it thickens, stirring all the time. Now pour it on the cake while the cake is still in the oven. Continue baking about 10 more minutes. The cinnamon icing should run into the batter so that it will be all through the cake. Delicious!

How to serve:

This is a color contrast cake. Put it on a glass plate with a pretty doily under it. You can put whipped cream over it to give it an extra richness, or you can put the whipped cream to the side in a small dish, so that those who choose to can add some after they have been given a slice. You can also just sprinkle some powdered sugar over it. Either way it is very good.

Fork-Only Buffet Dinners: Menu II

APPETIZERS: **Caviar Mousse**
(Can be done a day ahead)
Raw Vegetables Appetizer
(Can be done a day ahead)

MAIN DISHES: **Breasts of Chicken Continental**
(Can be done a day ahead)
Lobster and Chicken with Eggs
(Can be done a day ahead)
Cork-Shaped Meatballs
(Can be done a day ahead)
Zucchini and Tomatoes
(Can be done a day ahead)

SALAD: **Bacon and Lettuce Salad**
(Must be done the same day)

DESSERTS: **Thousand Leaves Cake**
(Can be done a day ahead)
Melon Balls with Mint
(Must be done the same day)

CAVIAR MOUSSE

(Can be done a day ahead) SERVES 8

Remember to use red caviar to prepare this most delicious appetizer. Black caviar turns gray but the red turns a beautiful, appetizing pink.

1 envelope plain gelatin (1 tablespoon)
2 tablespoons cold water
6-ounce jar red caviar
¼ cup chopped parsley
1 tablespoon chopped onion

1 teaspoon grated lemon peel
1 pint sour cream
1 cup whipped heavy cream
2 tablespoons hot water
½ teaspoon salt
½ teaspoon pepper
Lemon wedges for serving
Bunch of parsley for serving

Put the plain gelatin and the cold water in a small custard cup. Let the gelatin soak and soften.

Into a large bowl, put the caviar, parsley, onion, and lemon peel. Stir in the sour cream. In a small bowl, whip the heavy cream until stiff. Now add the hot water slowly to the gelatin and let it dissolve. When the gelatin has cooled enough, put it into the sour cream mixture. Then fold in the whipped heavy cream. Add the salt and pepper. Taste for additional seasoning. Spoon into a medium-sized soufflé dish or a ring mold. Chill.

Stop here if you are working ahead.

When preparing to serve the Caviar Mousse, unmold it by loosening it with a paring knife around the edges and turning it upside down.

How to serve:

If you are using a soufflé dish, unmold it onto a glass dish, and decorate with lemon wedges. Put a big sprig of parsley on top, right in the middle. If you are using a ring mold, circle it with lemon wedges and put a bunch of parsley in the middle.

Special hint: If you make this appetizer for a sit-down dinner, use 8 individual molds and serve on a bed of lettuce on individual dishes, decorated with a sprig of parsley and a lemon wedge.

RAW VEGETABLES APPETIZER
(Can be done a day ahead) SERVES 8

If you are going to have a heavy main dish and your appetizer is going to be eaten while your guests are sitting or standing around having drinks, the Raw Vegetables Appetizer will be great. It is best served with a Curry or Anchovy Mayonnaise. The vegetables that you choose should be unusual ones. Do not fall back on carrot and celery sticks. Be inventive. One good assortment is shown below.

1 fennel
2 red peppers
2 green peppers
½ pound mushrooms
1 head cauliflower
1 bunch broccoli
2 stalks Belgian endive
1 box cherry tomatoes
½ pound very fresh green beans
2 cucumbers
Curry or Anchovy Mayonnaise (see page 193)
Watercress or sprigs of parsley for serving
Rose radishes for serving

Most of these vegetables can be prepared a day ahead. However, the mushrooms and endive should be done at the last minute.

Wash the vegetables well. Be sure that they are served in convenient, bite-sized pieces. Cut the fennel and peppers into strips. Break the cauliflower into clusters of flowers, and cut the broccoli into half strips with the flower bud on top. Keep the cherry tomatoes and green beans whole. Cover well and chill in the refrigerator until almost serving time. Prepare the mayonnaise.

Stop here if you are working ahead.

When you are preparing to serve, do the mushrooms and the endive. The mushrooms can be kept whole or cut into slices. The endive need only be separated into leaves. Arrange all the vegetables. Then put the mayonnaise in the middle of your serving dish.

How to serve:
The larger the dish or plate the better. However, the plate should be either glass or wooden. Arrange the plate in an attractive way. Make sure that the dip dish is easy to get to. Keep small napkins nearby, just in case.

Special hint: Put watercress or sprigs of parsley somewhere around the dish to give it extra life. You can also use radish roses for extra color.

BREASTS OF CHICKEN CONTINENTAL
(Can be done a day ahead) SERVES 8

> 8 double chicken breasts with wing bones
> 1 tablespoon flour
> 2 tablespoons butter
> ¼ cup hot Marsala wine
> 2 tablespoons flour
> 1 tablespoon tomato paste
> 1 cup chicken stock
> 1 tablespoon salt
> 2 teaspoons pepper
> 1 teaspoon cayenne pepper
> 1 cup sour cream
> 2 tablespoons red currant jelly
> ¼ cup Parmesan cheese
> ½ stick butter (⅛ pound)
> 2 tablespoons chopped dill or parsley
> Bouquet of parsley for serving

Remove the meat from the bone, leaving a little of the wing bone. Split the breasts down the middle so that you have two singles from every double. Dust lightly with 1 tablespoon of flour. Melt the butter in a large skillet. When the butter is bubbly, add the chicken breasts, skin down, and brown quickly. Add hot Marsala wine. Remove the chicken and put it to the side. Mix 2 tablespoons flour into the fat; then add the tomato paste and chicken stock. Add salt, pepper, and cayenne pepper. Stir with a wooden spoon until the mixture becomes thick and smooth. Strain into a separate bowl. Put the chickens and gravy separately in the refrigerator.

Stop here if you are working ahead.

When preparing to serve, warm the chickens in the oven in a

foil-covered serving dish and put the gravy in a skillet. When the gravy is warm but *not hot*, very carefully add the sour cream little by little. Keep stirring until it is all used. Add the currant jelly. Pour the gravy over the chicken breasts. Sprinkle Parmesan cheese on top, add some chips of butter, and brown under the broiler.

How to serve:
Place the chicken breasts on the serving dish so that they are slightly overlapping. After they have been broiled, place a lamb frill on each chicken wing bone, sprinkle chopped parsley on top, and add a bouquet of parsley at one end of the dish.

LOBSTER AND CHICKEN WITH EGGS
(Can be done a day ahead)   SERVES 8

This chicken recipe costs more to make than others because of the lobster; but if you want to really impress your guests with an elegant and tasty dish, this is the dish to try.

1 stick butter (¼ pound)
2 three-pound-chickens cut up small
2 tablespoons brandy
4 tablespoons sherry
1 small chopped onion
4 medium-sized, skinned and sliced tomatoes
2 teaspoons tomato paste
4 tablespoons flour
2 cups chicken stock
5 medium-sized sliced mushrooms
¼ pound cooked lobster meat
1 teaspoon salt
1 teaspoon pepper
1 bay leaf
1 cup bread croutons
2 tablespoons butter
1 tablespoon vegetable oil
8 eggs
¼ cup freshly chopped chives or parsley

Melt the butter in a large skillet and then add the chicken. After 10 minutes turn the chicken onto the other side, cover, and cook very slowly for about 45 minutes. Remove the chicken pieces and put them into a dish to cool. Add the brandy and sherry to the butter and chicken drippings in the skillet. Stir slowly. Add the onions and tomatoes and cook for about 5 minutes. Stir in the tomato paste and flour and make sure they are blended. Add the chicken stock and bring it to a boil. Then remove it from the heat. Add the sliced mushrooms and the lobster meat. Season with salt and pepper and add the bay leaf. Pour the sauce into a separate bowl. Cool. Cover the cooled chicken pieces and sauce with foil and refrigerate.

Stop here if you are working ahead.

When preparing to serve, unwrap the chicken pieces and warm them in the oven with a little of the sauce. Brown the croutons separately in the butter. Put the rest of the sauce into a saucepan and heat to below boiling point. Put the vegetable oil into a large frying pan, and when the chicken is ready to be served, fry an egg for each serving.

How to serve:
Put the chicken pieces on a large shallow dish and pour the sauce all over it. Sprinkle the croutons over all. Place the fried eggs along the side of the dish and pour some more hot sauce over them. Sprinkle with chives or parsley.

It's delicious!

CORK-SHAPED MEATBALLS
(Can be done a day ahead)   SERVES 8

> 1½ pounds ground round steak
> 1½ cups buttermilk
> ½ cup rye bread crumbs
> 1 teaspoon salt
> ½ teaspoon pepper
> 1 tablespoon flour

½ stick butter (⅛ pound)
¼ cup olive oil
1 cup sour cream
4 tablespoons sherry
1 cup fresh mushroom stems
½ teaspoon paprika
Chopped parsley for serving

Blend together the ground round steak, buttermilk, bread crumbs, salt, and pepper in a large bowl. Take a scoop of the ground meat mixture in your hands and roll it in a little flour into the shape of a wine bottle cork. Not too small, not too large. When all the "corks" are ready, melt the butter in a large skillet. When the butter starts to bubble, put in the olive oil. Then put in the meatballs one by one. Do not allow them to get too well done. Put them to the side to cool. Combine the sour cream and the sherry and add the mixture to the skillet after it has been removed from the heat.

Put the skillet back on the heat and add the mushroom stems. Let the sauce cook for only 3 minutes. Do not let it boil. Take the sauce out of the pan and put it into a small bowl. Cool, wrap, and refrigerate it. Wrap the cooled, undercooked meatballs on their separate dish and put them into the refrigerator.

Stop here if you are working ahead.

When preparing to serve the Cork-Shaped Meatballs, remove the sauce from the refrigerator and let it remain at room temperature. Then, just before serving, heat the meatballs and the sauce in a skillet but *do not boil*. Add the paprika, and if you need additional flavoring or seasoning, add it now.

How to serve:
It's nice to serve this on a narrow shallow pan or dish, with the sauce poured over the meatballs and the chopped parsley sprinkled on top.

ZUCCHINI AND TOMATOES

(Can be done a day ahead)   SERVES 8

> 2 *pounds zucchini*
> 1 *cup cold water*
> 1 *teaspoon salt*
> 1 *teaspoon pepper*
> 2 *tablespoons vegetable oil*
> 2 *pounds medium-sized tomatoes*
> 1 *small clove crushed garlic*
> *Mornay Sauce (optional—see page 189)*

Wash and dry the zucchini. Then cut it into 1-inch thick pieces. Put it into the saucepan with the water and season with the salt and pepper. Cook until it comes to a boil, but do not overcook. Drain and put aside. Melt the vegetable oil in a small skillet. Cut tomatoes 1 inch thick and sauté for a minute or two on each side. Do not overcook. Remove from the pan and place each vegetable in the refrigerator in separate covered dishes.

Stop here if you are working ahead.

When you are preparing to serve Zucchini and Tomatoes, remove the vegetables from the refrigerator and keep them at room temperature for about ½ hour. Put them on a serving dish, with the zucchini on the bottom and the tomatoes on the top. Sprinkle with a little more salt and freshly ground pepper and the crushed garlic. Cover and warm in an oven at 350° for about 10 minutes.

How to serve:
When the Zucchini and Tomatoes are hot, you can bring them to the table, just as they are, or you can add Mornay Sauce.

BACON AND LETTUCE SALAD

(Must be done the same day)   SERVES 8

> 1 *head Boston lettuce*
> 1 *head Romaine lettuce*
> 1 *bunch watercress*

1 bunch chicory
2 pounds spinach leaves
6 slices diced bacon
2 tablespoons vinegar
¼ cup vegetable oil
1 teaspoon sugar
1 teaspoon freshly ground pepper
Pinch salt

Wash and dry very carefully the Boston and Romaine lettuce, watercress, chicory, and spinach leaves. Wrap in paper towels and keep in the refrigerator. Fry diced bacon in a skillet, but do not burn it. Drain. Put the vinegar, oil, sugar, pepper, and salt into a small bowl or into a screw-top jar. Shake and store.

How to serve:

Put the lettuce and the greens into a dish or bowl. Be sure to break the lettuce leaves rather than cut them. Shake and pour the dressing over the greens. Sprinkle on the bacon chips and serve. It's unusual and tasty!

THOUSAND LEAVES CAKE

(Can be done a day ahead)   SERVES 8

This is the closest thing to a puff pastry dough in taste without the hard work of puff pastry.

Crust:

1 pound butter
1⅔ cups sifted flour
4 tablespoons ice water
Granulated sugar

Put the butter and flour into a bowl and crumble it with your fingers until it looks like cornmeal. Add the ice water slowly, mixing with a fork. Pick up the dough and make a small mound out of it. Wrap it in wax paper and refrigerate.

Stop here if you are working ahead.

When ready to use, divide the dough into 6 or 7 portions. Preheat the oven to 450°. Take a long strip of wax paper and use a pencil to mark off the size of circle you want. You can use a plate, a large pot lid, a salad bowl, anything. Cut out, depending on size, enough to use all the dough. Thinly roll out the divided portion onto the cut circle. Prick with a fork and sprinkle some ice water and some granulated sugar on it. Put it on a cookie sheet and bake in the oven for at least 10 minutes until golden brown. Remove from the oven, but keep it on wax paper until it is cool (only a little while). Keep the crust on the plate and cover with foil to keep dry.

When preparing to serve, make the Vanilla Cream Filling.

Vanilla cream filling:

2 egg yolks
1½ tablespoons butter
1 tablespoon potato flour
1 cup light cream or half-and-half
2 tablespoons sugar
1 teaspoon vanilla extract
Applesauce

Mix the egg yolks, butter, potato flour, light cream, and sugar in top of double boiler until smooth and thick—stirring all the time. Remove from heat and cool. Then add the vanilla extract.

Spread alternate layers of commercial applesauce and the vanilla cream. The top will be crust, on which you can put an icing or some sweetened whipped cream. If you use icing, the following is a good recipe.

Icing:

1 cup powdered sugar
1½ tablespoons water
½ tablespoon lemon juice
Chopped walnuts for serving

Put the sugar, water, and lemon juice into bowl and stir until melted. Spread on top of the cake with a spoon.

How to serve:

This cake will not look as pretty as you might want it to look. It is so delicious, though, that all you have to do is decorate it a little. Put it on a cake platter. If you use the icing on top, in a small glass bowl have some extra whipped cream to spoon on after wedges have been cut. I have seen fresh flowers put alongside it. It's also a good idea to sprinkle chopped walnuts on the top and sides after the cake is iced.

MELON BALLS WITH MINT

(Must be done the same day)   SERVES 8

This is a very refreshing dessert, a summertime must. It is also very good in the winter except that, in certain parts of the country, melons are both difficult to find and expensive.

Melons
Crème de menthe
Sprig of fresh mint

You can use honeydew melon, Persian melon, cantaloupe, casaba, and/or watermelon.

You can use just one melon, or a combination of two or three. Always chill the melons before you scoop out the balls. After you have scooped out the amount you want, put the balls into a glass bowl. Squeeze out the natural juices from the remaining pulp and core. Refrigerate the melon balls and juice separately until ready to be served.

How to serve:

Whether you are putting them into individual goblets or into one large glass bowl, start with the melon balls and add the natural juices, a dash of crème de menthe and on top of that a sprig of fresh mint.

Special hint: You can also use dried mint if you marinate it with crème de menthe first.

Fork-Only Buffet Dinners: Menu III

APPETIZERS: Aspic Mousse of Salmon
               (Can be done a day ahead)
               Roquefort Spread and Hot Chips
               (Can be done a day ahead)
MAIN DISHES: Ragout of Veal
               (Can be done a day ahead)
               Meat Loaves en Croute with a Spicy Sauce
               (Can be done a day ahead)
               Caneton à L'Orange
               (Can be done a day ahead)
               Baked Kale Gruyère
               (Can be done a day ahead)
SALADS: Cold Vegetable Salad
               (Can be done a day ahead)
               Mixed Green Salad
               (Can be done a day ahead)
DESSERTS: Peaches in Blankets
               (Must be started 2 days ahead)
               Cold Chocolate Mousse
               (Can be done a day ahead)

ASPIC MOUSSE OF SALMON
(Can be done a day ahead)   SERVES 8

On a fork-only buffet table, it is a must to have a cold mousse of some kind. This is a delicious one, and it is great for any time. It is also good in that you do most of the work the day before and just put the finishing touches on before you serve it.

2 tablespoons gelatin
2 tablespoons cold water

2 tablespoons hot water
2½ cups cooked cold salmon
⅓ cup lemon juice
1 tablespoon chopped parsley
1 teaspoon Tabasco sauce
1 teaspoon Worcestershire sauce
1 cup mayonnaise
Salt to taste
2 large peeled cucumbers for serving
Lemon slices for serving
Parsley for serving

Put the gelatin into the cold water and let it set; then dissolve it slowly with the hot water. Into a bowl put the cold, flaked salmon, lemon juice, parsley, Tabasco sauce, Worcestershire sauce, mayonnaise, and salt. Add the gelatin and mix carefully but thoroughly. Place in a mold of your choosing. Refrigerate.

Stop here if you are working ahead.

When ready to serve, unmold onto small leaves of lettuce.

How to serve:

I like to unmold aspic dishes on glass plates or on big silver ones. Cut the cucumbers into slices about ½ inch thick. Season the cucumbers and put them all around the salmon mousse. Place lemon slices in between the cucumbers and little flowerettes of parsley next to the lemon. It's attractive and delicious.

ROQUEFORT SPREAD AND HOT CHIPS

(Can be done a day ahead)   SERVES 8

¼ pound Roquefort cheese
½ cup heavy cream (not too watery)
1 drop Tabasco sauce
Tiny pinch cayenne pepper
4 slices dark rye bread cut into fingers
1 pound potato chips
Parsley or watercress for serving

Mash the Roquefort cheese with a fork and add the heavy cream, a little at a time, to soften it. You might need less than ½ cup or a tiny bit more—it depends on the smoothness you like. Put in the Tabasco sauce and the cayenne pepper. Mix until well blended. Put into refrigerator.

Stop here if you are working ahead.

When preparing to serve, take the Roquefort cheese mixture out and put it to the side. Cut the rye bread into fingers and mound the softened cheese on them. Don't be stingy with it. While you are doing the spreading, put the potato chips into an oven-proof dish and set them in the oven to get very hot and crispy.

How to serve:
Put the cheese fingers on a glass plate or a wooden tray. You can line them up, make them into a zig-zag pattern, or arrange them almost any way you want. Put the hot chips at either end of the tray or plate, or if you like, in an attractive individual bowl. If you serve the chips in an individual bowl, be sure to use parsley or watercress around the cheese strips for added color.

RAGOUT OF VEAL

(Can be done a day ahead)   SERVES 8

A ragout, or stew as some people call it, can be done in a very delicious way and be used as an elegant dinner dish. This is a hearty meal to which the delicate flavor of the veal gives added interest.

4 pounds veal from the leg cut into 1-inch squares
1 quart water
2 teaspoons salt
2 teaspoons pepper
1 teaspoon paprika
3 carrots cut into large chunks
2 medium-sized onions with 2 cloves in each

Bouquet garni
1 tablespoon butter
12 small onions
½ pound mushrooms

Put the cut up veal, water, salt, pepper, and paprika into a deep pot. Bring to a boil.

Remove scum from the top and add the carrots, the medium-sized onions studded with cloves, and the bouquet garni (thyme, sage, and bay leaf in a cheesecloth bag). Simmer for 1 hour, or until tender. Do not allow to boil. While the stock is being cooked, melt the butter in a small skillet and add the small onions and mushrooms. Fry for a minute or two, and then put aside to cool. When the veal is cooked, take it off the heat and remove it from the pot. Pour all the stock into a large bowl and cool. Refrigerate. Wrap the meat and refrigerate. Refrigerate the onions and mushrooms in a small dish.

Stop here if you are working ahead.

Sauce:

1 cup strained veal stock
4 tablespoons butter
2 tablespoons flour
3 beaten egg yolks
½ cup cream
¼ cup sherry

When you are preparing to serve, unwrap the meat, remove the layer of fat that will have settled on the stock, and put the stock into a saucepan to warm. In a skillet melt the butter; stir in the flour, add the strained veal stock, and cook until thick. Throw away the bouquet garni. Remove the sauce from the heat. Mix the beaten egg yolks with the cream and add them to the sauce. Add more stock if you need it. Taste for seasoning. Save the carrots from the original stock. Add the onions, mushrooms, carrots, and meat to the now-thickened sauce. It should be thick, not runny. Let the meat absorb the sauce flavor. Add the sherry and let all of the flavors blend.

How to serve:

Put into a deep dish or pan and sprinkle a little paprika on top for color. Serve with rice.

MEAT LOAVES *EN CROUTE* WITH A SPICY SAUCE
(Can be done a day ahead) SERVES 8

This is a basically simple dish but this recipe with the *en croute* makes it unusual and the spicy sauce makes it delicious. It is perfect for your fork-only table.

3 pounds ground beef
1 pound ground pork
2 pounds ground veal
1 medium-sized chopped onion
1 tablespoon chopped parsley
2 tablespoons chopped green pepper
1 tablespoon ground pepper
1 tablespoon salt
2 whole eggs
½ cup pieces stale white bread
¼ cup red wine
Sprigs of parsley or watercress for serving

Preheat the oven to 375'. Put the beef, pork, veal, onion, parsley, green pepper, pepper, and salt into a large bowl. Put the stale pieces of bread and the whole eggs into a small bowl. Use a fork to mix the eggs and bread together until the bread is completely soaked. Put the egg and bread mixture into the large bowl of meat. Add the red wine and stir with a fork until all is blended. Shape into one large or two small loaves. Place on a shallow greased pan and put into the oven for about 30 minutes. (You want it to be underdone, since the cooking process will continue when the crust is put on.) Remove and put to the side to cool. Refrigerate. Then make the crust.

Crust:
5 cups sifted flour
2 teaspoons salt

1½ cup vegetable shortening or lard
½ cup ice water
¼ cup egg wash (egg white mixed with a little water)

Sift flour into a bowl. Then add the salt and shortening. Cut with two knives or a pastry blender. The dough should have a thick, bread crumb consistency. Add the ice water and gather the dough with a fork, mixing all the time. Form a ball, wrap in wax paper, and refrigerate until ready to use. Make the sauce.

Sauce:

1 cup catsup
1 teaspoon chili powder
1 tablespoon seasoned salt
½ cup vinegar
2 tablespoons Worcestershire sauce
2 teaspoons Dijon mustard
Few drops Tabasco sauce

Put all of the ingredients into a small bowl or a screw-top jar and blend them together. This is a sauce you can use to baste the baking meat loaves, but for meat loaves *en croute* it's best served on the side.

Stop here if you are working ahead.

About an hour before serving time, preheat the oven to 350° and roll out the crust very thin. Place the crust over the meat loaf, tucking it in at the bottom and sides. Prick the crust on top in several places with a fork and brush it with the egg wash to make the top brown nicely. The dish is ready when the crust is cooked and slightly brown.

How to serve:

If you have made two loaves, slightly slant them when you display them. The sauce should be nearby. If you have made the mixture into one large loaf, put it on a large platter with the sauce nearby and decorate with sprigs of parsley or watercress on each end.

CANETON À L'ORANGE
(Can be done a day ahead)   SERVES 8

Very few people know how to really cook a duck. The following way is perfection and it will be juicy and flavorful. This makes
an excellent buffet dish, since it is tender enough to be on your
fork-only menu. For real elegance, serve this also at your sit-down
dinners.

2 four-pound ducks, cut up (ask the butcher to do it for you)
1 stick butter (¼ pound)
2 tablespoons hot Marsala wine
1 small clove crushed garlic
4 small chopped mushrooms
2 tablespoons shredded orange rind (save the orange for serving)
1 teaspoon tomato paste
1 teaspoon meat glaze
2 tablespoons potato flour
1½ cups stock
¼ cup red wine
2 tablespoons orange juice
1 teaspoon salt
1 teaspoon pepper
1 small bay leaf
1 teaspoon red currant jelly

Brown the cut up pieces of duck in the hot butter. If you have
too much fat after browning, drain it off, saving only 3 tablespoons.
Pour the Marsala wine over the duck. Remove the duck from the
pan. Add the crushed garlic and the chopped mushrooms to the
pan, and sauté for about 2 minutes. Then add the shredded orange
rind and cook for another 2 minutes. Add the tomato paste, meat
glaze, and potato flour. Stir until it makes a paste. Add the stock,
red wine, and orange juice. Stir until it boils, and then add the salt,
pepper, bay leaf, and red currant jelly. Cool and put on the side.
Cover the duck in foil and cool. Put the gravy and the duck pieces
in the refrigerator.

Stop here if you are working ahead.

When preparing to serve, take the stock and put it into a large pot. When it is warm, add the duck pieces. Put a piece of wax paper on top and cover with a lid. Cook for at least 45 minutes, stirring frequently.

How to serve:

Arrange the duck in a casserole and add the sauce. Take the orange that you peeled for the sauce and slice it. Arrange the slices around the duck. Serve. This is delicious!

BAKED KALE GRUYÈRE

(Can be done a day ahead)   SERVES 8

To find and then prepare and serve unusual vegetables is a challenge. Kale is such an unusual vegetable and the following recipe is particularly good to use for your buffet table.

3 pounds kale
1 quart water
1 tablespoon salt
1 cup Mornay Sauce
2 tablespoons finely chopped Gruyère cheese
1 teaspoon sesame seeds

Wash the tender leaves of the kale. Discard the imperfect leaves and the tough midribs. Drain well. Put the kale, water, and salt into a large pot. Cover tightly and boil steadily for 15 minutes. Drain and chop fine. Keep it warm if you are going to use it soon; otherwise, put it into a bowl, cool, cover, and refrigerate.

Stop here if you are working ahead.

Remove the dish from the refrigerator and keep it at room temperature for at least ½ hour before serving. To get it very hot, just put some salted water in a pot, put in the kale, and cook for about 1 minute. Drain. Cover with Mornay Sauce (see page 189). Sprinkle with 2 tablespoons finely chopped Gruyère cheese. Put under broiler until it is slightly browned.

How to serve:

I like to serve this vegetable in a pretty copper pan sprinkled with some sesame seeds.

COLD VEGETABLE SALAD

(Can be done a day ahead)   SERVES 8

1 cup diced carrots
1 cup beets (fresh or canned)
1 small cauliflower
1 cup green beans
4 artichoke hearts
1 cup fresh green peas

1 large head lettuce
½ cup chili sauce
1 cup mayonnaise
½ teaspoon paprika
1 tablespoon lemon juice
½ teaspoon celery salt
Pinch chopped tarragon

Cook each vegetable separately. Do not overcook them. They should taste firm when you bite them—not mushy. After the beets have been cooked, dice them. The cauliflower should be pulled apart into clusters and then cooked quickly. The green beans are best in this salad if they are cut into long strips. The artichoke hearts should be cut in half.

Wash the lettuce carefully and remove any wilted leaves. Dry with paper towels. Cover the lettuce with a dampened towel and put it into the refrigerator. Do the same with the vegetables, but wrap or cover them with foil.

Stop here if you are working ahead.

Just before you are ready to serve them, take the lettuce leaves and put them around the sides and bottom of the bowl. Group the vegetables on the lettuce, arranged by color, texture, and size. Mix the chili sauce, mayonnaise, paprika, lemon juice, and celery salt with a fork until blended. Pour the dressing over the vegetables. Sprinkle the chopped fresh tarragon over the dressing.

How to serve:
Even though most everyone likes to serve this in a big bowl, I like to serve it on a long, shallow dish. I find it is very eye-appealing that way.

MIXED GREEN SALAD
(Can be done a day ahead)   SERVES 8

> 2 heads Boston lettuce
> 1 bunch romaine lettuce
> 1 bunch escarole
> 1 peeled and sliced cucumber
> 2 medium-sized skinned tomatoes
> Salt
> Pepper
> ½ cup vegetable oil
> ¼ cup vinegar
> 1 teaspoon salt
> 1 teaspoon pepper
> ½ teaspoon dry hot mustard
> Sliced fresh mushrooms (optional)

Wash and throw away the wilted and dead leaves of the Boston, romaine, and escarole. To keep it fresh and crisp when you prepare it the day before, wrap it in paper towels or a cotton dishtowel and put it into the refrigerator. Cut up the cucumbers, put them into small bowl, add a little salt and pepper and refrigerate. Peel the tomatoes (see page 7) but do not cut them up yet. Put them in a small dish and cut them just before you mix the entire salad.

Stop here if you are working ahead.

When you are preparing to serve the salad, put the greens into a large wooden bowl. Cut up and add the tomatoes and cucumbers.

Mix the oil, vinegar, salt, pepper, and mustard in a screw-top jar. Taste, shake, and pour over the salad. Mix it around with your hands or a salad fork and spoon.

How to serve:
Use a large wooden bowl or a pretty glass bowl.

Special hint: I also like to add fresh mushrooms, cleaned and sliced, to this salad.

PEACHES IN BLANKETS

(Must be started 2 days ahead)   SERVES 8

Crust:
Start the crust at least 2 weeks ahead if you intend to freeze it, or 2 days ahead if you intend to refrigerate it.

1 stick softened butter (¼ pound)
1 whole egg
2 egg yolks
¼ cup sugar
2½ cups flour
1 tablespoon ice water

In a bowl beat butter, whole egg, egg yolks, and sugar, until well blended. Sift the flour and add to the mixture, using a wooden spoon. Add the water a little at a time until all is blended. Wrap in wax paper or foil. Freeze or refrigerate.

Stop here if you are working ahead.

Hard sauce:
This sauce goes well with Peaches in Blankets. It can be made a day before.

½ stick softened butter (¼ pound)
1 whole egg
2 cups powdered sugar
1 teaspoon almond flavoring
½ teaspoon powdered nutmeg
Whipped heavy cream

Cream the butter, add the whole egg, and mix well. Slowly add the powdered sugar. It will now be almost thick. Add the almond flavoring and sprinkle with nutmeg. Refrigerate.

Stop here if you are working ahead.

When you are ready to use the sauce, add a little whipped heavy cream to it. It will make it a little more runny.

How to serve:
8 fresh, ripe, medium-sized peaches. *

Remove dough crust in time for it to soften and be in workable condition. Roll the dough out on lightly floured board to the thickness you want. Cut strips as long as needed to cover the peaches all around. Pat gently to seal. Brush a little milk on top of crust to brown. Put into oven of 400° when you sit down to dinner. They will take about 30 minutes. Remove and keep warm. Serve on a big round plate, garnishing with the hard sauce on top.

* If peaches are not in season, you can use apples.

COLD CHOCOLATE MOUSSE
(Can be done a day ahead)   SERVES 8

>   *6 ounces semi-sweet dark chocolate*
>   *2 tablespoons water*
>   *3 tablespoons already brewed coffee*
>   *1 stick butter*
>   *6 separated eggs*
>   *½ pint whipped heavy cream*
>   *5 tablespoons fine sugar*
>   *Cocoa for serving*
>   *Powdered sugar for serving*
>   *Extra whipped heavy cream*

In the top part of a double boiler, melt the chocolate in the water with the coffee over hot, not boiling, water. While the mixture is still warm, put in the butter. Cool. Beat the egg yolks until frothy, and then add them to the cooled chocolate mixture. Whip the heavy cream until it forms peaks. Add the sugar. Beat the egg whites until stiff. Then fold the egg whites and heavy cream into the chocolate mixture. Pour this into a soufflé dish. Refrigerate at least 5 hours; overnight is still better.

Stop here if you are working ahead.

How to serve:

Be sure to serve the mousse in a typically white soufflé dish placed on a silver platter or a wooden tray. On top of the mousse you should sprinkle some cocoa and then some powdered sugar. A few paper doilies around the mousse show it off well. Scoop it into individual glass bowls with a large spoon so that, even when you put it into the dish, it has a clean cut, not a messy, look to it. Serve with extra whipped cream on top.

8 ᘓ

Knife-and-Fork Buffet Dinners

Knife-and-Fork Buffet Dinners: Menu I

APPETIZERS:	Eggs with Sour Cream and Vegetables *(Can be done a day ahead)*
	Cold Shrimp Superb *(Can be done a day ahead)*
	Cucumbered Fish Mousse *(Can be done a day ahead)*
MAIN DISHES:	Party Pork Dish *(Can be done a day ahead)*
	Chicken Sweet and Spicy *(Can be done a day ahead)*
	Filet Strips of Beef with Herb Butter *(Can be done 2 days ahead)*
	Carrots with Grapes *(Can be done a day ahead)*
SALAD:	Mixed Green Salad *(Can be done a day ahead)*

DESSERTS: Hazelnut Pudding à la Creme
(Can be done a day ahead)
French Strawberry Cake
(Can be done a day ahead)

EGGS WITH SOUR CREAM AND VEGETABLES

(Can be done a day ahead)   SERVES 8

6 hard-boiled eggs
1 package frozen mixed vegetables
1 tablespoon salt
2 teaspoons freshly ground pepper
1 teaspoon paprika
¼ cup mayonnaise
¼ cup sour cream
1 can flat anchovy fillets
1 teaspoon capers
Parsley for serving

Hard boil the eggs, but keep them in their shells. Cook the frozen mixed vegetables very quickly—about 2 minutes—and while they are still crisp, drain and put them aside to cool. When cool, put the vegetables and the unshelled hard-boiled eggs into the refrigerator.

Stop here if you are working ahead.

On the day of the party, shell the eggs. Using an egg slicer, slice the eggs (keeping them in shape) and transfer them to a serving plate. Put the mixed vegetables around the eggs. Sprinkle the salt, pepper, and paprika onto the eggs and vegetables.

Mix the mayonnaise and sour cream in a small bowl until the mixture is runny but not too thin. Spoon as much as you want of this mixture over the eggs and the vegetables, but make sure you use enough to cover them.

Take the anchovy strips and put them on top of the eggs in any design you want. Sprinkle the capers over all.

How to serve:

Serve this dish as it is now arranged on the plate. Add a bouquet of parsley on either side to add color.

COLD SHRIMP SUPERB

(Can be done a day ahead)   SERVES 8

Everytime I want an appetizer that would be delicious and unusual, I think of this one. It can be done the day before and its taste is biting enough to whet your appetite for the meal to come.

2 pounds raw shrimp
2 medium-sized finely chopped onions
1 medium-sized finely chopped garlic clove
2 tablespoons vegetable oil
1 teaspoon vinegar
1 teaspoon salt
1 teaspoon mustard
2 tablespoons horseradish
Pinch sage
Lemon slices for serving
Pinch chopped parsley for serving

Put the shrimp into just enough water to cover and cook them until they turn pink or light red. Remove, and allow the shrimp to cool before shelling and deveining. While the shrimp are cooking and cooling, chop the onion and garlic. Put the chopped onion and garlic into a bowl or screw-top jar with the oil, vinegar, salt, mustard, horseradish, and sage. Taste for added seasoning. Shake well and put into the bowl with the shrimp.

How to serve:

This dish should be served cold. I like to see it in a pretty, shallow glass bowl. Place the shrimp in the dish with slices of lemon around it and, if you want, a little chopped parsley on top. Use fancy toothpicks for the top shrimp only.

CUCUMBERED FISH MOUSSE
(Can be done a day ahead) SERVES 8

This very good fish mousse is not too difficult to prepare, but once it is decorated, it is impressive on the table. It can be sensational in the summer, but I often serve it at a winter party also.

1 pound haddock
2 pounds flounder
2 cups water
½ cup white wine
1 slice lemon
1 bay leaf
½ teaspoon pepper

1 cup mayonnaise
½ cup whipped heavy cream
2 tablespoons lemon juice
1 teaspoon Worcestershire sauce
3 tablespoons chopped parsley
2 tablespoons seasoned salt
2 envelopes plain gelatin (2 tablespoons)
2 tablespoons cold water
2 tablespoons warm water
Dash Tabasco sauce
2 peeled and thinly sliced cucumbers
Lettuce for serving
Small tomatoes for serving
Cluster of parsley or watercress for serving

Preheat the oven to 350°. Put a cake rack into a shallow pan. Put the haddock and flounder on the rack and add the water, wine, lemon, bay leaf, and pepper. Baste the fish every so often until it is tender. Remove the fish and let it stand in the stock until cool. Drain and save the stock. Flake the fish and remove the bones and skin. You should have about 6 cups of fish.

In a large bowl mix the mayonnaise, whipped heavy cream, lemon juice, Worcestershire sauce, parsley, seasoned salt, and ½ cup of cooled fish stock. Taste to see if you need more salt. Add the fish and beat together in a blender until well mixed and smooth.

Taste and add more seasoning if necessary. Soak the gelatin in the cold water for about 2 minutes; then dissolve it in the warm water. Add the Tabasco sauce and the dissolved gelatin to the fish mixture. Get a large ring mold and rinse it with cold water. Do not dry the mold. Take the cucumber slices and place them on the bottom and sides of the mold. Pour the fish mixture into the mold. Chill.

Stop here if you are working ahead.

When preparing to serve, finely shred a few leaves of lettuce and put them on a large glass plate. Take a paring knife and run a little hot water over the blade. With the warmed knife, loosen the sides of the mold. Turn the mold upside down onto the shredded lettuce. If it does not turn out quickly, take a warm towel, and just for a minute, put it on the mold to loosen it. Put the whole plate in the refrigerator for at least an hour before serving to absorb any moisture from the warmed towel or knife.

How to serve:

The prettiest way to display this dish on a buffet table is to use tiny tomatoes. Keep the tomatoes whole, wash and cut the bottoms so they will sit flat, and keep the stems on. Circle the sides of the fish mold with the tomatoes, and in the middle of the ring mold, put a cluster of parsley or watercress. It's a pretty combination of white, green, and red.

PARTY PORK DISH
(Can be done a day ahead)   SERVES 8

Pork dishes are delicious. This one is good to eat and appealing to look at. It will look great on a buffet table for your knife-and-fork party.

> *6 pounds boned loin pork*
> *½ tablespoon salt*
> *1 teaspoon ground pepper*
> *¼ cup pineapple juice*

Preheat oven to 375°. Salt and pepper the pork and pour the pineapple juice over the top.

Put into a roasting pan and roast for 1½ hours. Remove, set aside to cool, and then refrigerate.

Stop here if you are working ahead.

Sauce:

1 stick sweet butter (¼ pound)
1 teaspoon dried crushed tarragon
1 tablespoon tomato paste
2 teaspoons meat concentrate
4 tablespoons potato flour
1 cup red Dubonnet
½ cup pineapple juice
1 cup chicken stock
1 teaspoon salt
1 teaspoon cayenne pepper
2 tablespoons salted butter
8 medium-sized mushrooms
1 small crushed clove garlic
8 small tomatoes
8 slices canned pineapple
Bouquet of parsley for serving

Take the pork which has been cooked and slice it into one-inch thicknesses. Melt the butter in a large skillet, and when it is hot, put in the slices of pork and brown them on both sides. Remove the pork and put the slices on a serving dish. Add the tarragon to the skillet. Remove the skillet from the heat and add the tomato paste, meat concentrate, and potato flour. Stir until the ingredients are mixed. Put the skillet back on low heat and add slowly the red Dubonnet, pineapple juice, and chicken stock. Stir constantly to the boiling point. It will be slightly thickened. Add the salt and cayenne pepper. In another small pan, melt the salted butter and sauté the mushrooms, crushed garlic, and small tomatoes for only a couple of minutes. Add this to the other gravy.

On your serving dish, overlap the pork slices (make sure they are warm) and pour the hot sauce over them, allowing the mushrooms and tomatoes to fall where they will. Take the pineapple slices and put them on top. Just before you put this dish on your

table, put it under the broiler to brown the pineapple. Serve very
hot.

How to serve:

In the middle of each browned pineapple slice, I put a fancy
toothpick with a lamb frill on it. On the ends of the serving tray I
put a bouquet of parsley. This is an unusually attractive dish to
serve and very good to eat.

CHICKEN SWEET AND SPICY

(Can be done a day ahead)   SERVES 8

This recipe is good for a knife-and-fork party or for a "Company Coming for Dinner" menu.

> 2 tablespoons bacon fat
> 2 three-pound chickens cut up into 8 pieces each
> 2 tablespoons sherry
> 2 teaspoons tomato paste
> 1 teaspoon meat glaze
> 5 level teaspoons potato flour
> 2 cups chicken stock
> 2 sprigs tarragon
> 2 sprigs parsley
> 1 tablespoon salt
> 2 teaspoons pepper
> 2 tablespoons butter
> 2 tablespoons olive oil
> 2 teaspoons chopped garlic
> 5 sliced mushrooms
> 3 tablespoons diced red pepper
> 3 tablespoons diced green pepper
> 2 skinned and quartered tomatoes
> Grated orange rind
> Orange slices and swirls

Melt the bacon fat in a large skillet and brown the small pieces
of chicken in it. When the chicken is browned, add the sherry and

cook for only about a minute. Remove the chicken, but keep it warm. Add the tomato paste, meat glaze, and potato flour to the skillet. Stir and blend well. Add the chicken stock. Stir slowly and cook carefully. The mixture will be nice and thick. Return the chicken to the skillet and add the tarragon, parsley, salt, and pepper. Cover and cook for 1 hour. Put to the side and allow to cool. Refrigerate.

Stop here if you are working ahead.

When you are preparing to serve, warm the chicken in the sauce until it is hot, but do not boil it. Keep it hot and watch it. Melt the butter in another small skillet. Add the olive oil, garlic, and mushrooms and sauté for about 5 minutes. Add the red and green peppers and the quartered tomatoes, and then the grated orange rind. Cook all of this for about 10 minutes.

How to serve:
Place the chicken with the sauce in a serving dish. Put the orange slices on top of the sauce. Then pour the green and red pepper sauce over all of that. For added effect, put swirls of orange on top.

FILET STRIPS OF BEEF WITH HERB BUTTER
(Can be done 2 days ahead)   SERVES 8

This is an excellent dish for a knife-and-fork supper or a buffet dinner. The reason I like it so much is because the beef is cut into strips that are easy to handle, and when served with your other dishes on the buffet table, it is appetizing and eye appealing. Try this the next time you have a large group over.

½ stick butter (⅛ pound)
2 medium-sized finely chopped onions
1 pound small mushrooms
2 tablespoons flour
¼ cup red wine
½ cup of beef bouillon stock

8 slices tenderloin beef cut into 1-inch thick strips
2 tablespoons flour
¼ cup bread crumbs
2 teaspoons salt
1 teaspoon pepper
Bouquet of watercress or parsley for serving

Take the butter out to soften it. Chop the onions and clean the mushrooms. Melt the butter in a skillet. Add the onions and sauté them until golden. Add the mushrooms and cook for 2 minutes more. Sprinkle with 2 tablespoons flour to thicken, and then add the wine and stock. Remove the onion-mushroom gravy and refrigerate.

Roll the strips of beef in a mixture of the remaining flour, bread crumbs, salt, and pepper. Fry in butter in skillet very quickly. Remove, cool, and refrigerate.

Herb butter:

1 stick butter (¼ pound)
1 teaspoon chopped parsley
1 teaspoon chopped thyme
1 teaspoon chopped rosemary

Put the butter in a small bowl and allow it to soften. Add the chopped parsley, thyme, and rosemary, and stir. Put into the refrigerator until ready to use.

Stop here if you are working ahead.

When you are preparing to serve, heat the gravy in the skillet. Add more butter if necessary. Then add the beef strips and get them very hot.

How to serve:

I prefer to show off the beef on an oval copper pan, decorated on each end with a bouquet of watercress or parsley. Just before bringing to the table, put chips of the herb butter all over the beef and allow them to melt. Delicious.

CARROTS WITH GRAPES
(Can be done a day ahead)   SERVES 8

Vegetables are difficult to serve on a buffet table but Carrots with Grapes is unusual and tasty. If you know someone who does not like carrots, have him try this tasty mouthful. He will be converted immediately.

> *1 stick butter (¼ pound)*
> *2 medium-sized bunches of carrots peeled and cut into thick, diagonal slices*
> *1 teaspoon sugar*
> *1 tablespoon vodka*
> *1 cup water*
> *Salt and pepper to taste*
> *½ pound seedless green grapes*
> *Chopped parsley for serving*

Melt the butter in a skillet and sauté carrots for about 5 minutes. Sprinkle the carrots with the sugar and cook for another 5 minutes. Add the vodka, water, and salt and pepper to taste. Cook until almost tender. Cool and put the vegetables and ½ of their juice into a bowl. Refrigerate.

Stop here if you are working ahead.

When you are preparing to serve, heat the carrots in the juice you saved. Add a little more butter if needed. When the carrots are good and hot, add the grapes. Leave in a few seconds.

How to serve:
Serve in a copper dish. Sprinkle with chopped parsley.

MIXED GREEN SALAD
(Can be done a day ahead)   SERVES 8

> *1 bunch watercress*
> *1 bunch romaine lettuce*
> *Small head Boston lettuce*

Clean the watercress, romaine lettuce, and Boston lettuce. Dry them with paper towels. Break the lettuce into small pieces and make sure the watercress is off the stems. Put all the greens into a clean paper bag. Refrigerate.

Stop here if you are working ahead.

Dressing:
The best type of dressing to serve on a simple green salad is oil and vinegar.

½ cup oil
4 tablespoons wine vinegar
2 teaspoons salt
1 teaspoon ground pepper
½ teaspoon sugar
½ teaspoon dry hot mustard

Put all the ingredients into a screw-top jar and shake well before serving. The important thing to remember when you pour the dressing on the salad is don't pour too much. Add the dressing little by little and keep tossing so that each piece of green has some dressing on it. Make sure you have no dressing at the bottom of the salad bowl.

Helpful Hint: If you do find that you have put too much dressing on the salad, take some paper towels and pat here and there to absorb the excess.

HAZELNUT PUDDING À LA CREME
(Can be done a day ahead)   SERVES 8

1 tablespoon plain gelatin
1 tablespoon cold water
1 tablespoon hot water
8 ounces blanched and skinned hazelnuts
2½ cups light cream or half-and-half
½ cup fine sugar
4 separated eggs
Pinch salt

1 teaspoon almond extract
1½ cups whipped heavy cream
2 tablespoons powdered sugar
A few whole hazelnuts for serving
Extra whipped heavy cream for serving

Soak the gelatin in the cold water. When it sets, dissolve it very slowly in the hot water. Put to the side. Pound the hazelnuts with a heavy mallet or even the bottom of a frying pan. Set aside. Put the light cream and the sugar into a small pan and bring to a boil. When the sugar has dissolved, turn off the heat. Beat the egg yolks and very carefully add them to the now cooled, but not cold, light cream–sugar mixture. Slowly bring the mixture to a boil, stirring constantly until it thickens. Remove from the heat and add the dissolved gelatin and a pinch of salt. Allow to cool on the side— do not put into the refrigerator because it will set if you do. While it is cooling, beat the egg whites until stiff. Add beaten egg whites to the cooled pudding, folding in carefully. Add the almond extract and fold in the pounded nuts. Place it all in either tall glasses or a shallow crystal bowl. Refrigerate.

Stop here if you are working ahead.

When preparing to serve, whip the heavy cream and add the powdered sugar. Make rosettes to decorate, and on each rosette, place a whole hazelnut. Or, put only one large hazelnut in the middle, and ground hazelnuts around the sides.

How to serve:
This dish can be displayed on the Buffet Table in a big glass bowl with an additional small bowl of whipped cream next to it. It's so very pretty to look at and it's delicious! Good for both spring and winter, although I like it more in winter.

FRENCH STRAWBERRY CAKE
(Can be done a day ahead)   SERVES 8

When it comes to desserts, always have a variety. This dish is most unusual, but it is a very delicious cake for your buffet table.

Your guests will not ask you where you bought it, but they will ask you for your recipe.

Cake:
6 egg whites
4 tablespoons ground walnuts
1 cup granulated sugar
½ cup sifted flour

Preheat the oven to 375°. Cut 3 circles, about 9 inches around, out of wax paper. Grease and lightly flour 2 cookie sheets. On the cookie sheets, mark 3 circles, about 9 inches around. Put the wax circles on the cookie sheets.

Beat the egg whites stiffly. Add the ground walnuts and sugar and fold in the sifted flour. Divide this mixture into 3 parts and spread with a spatula onto the 3 circles. Put into the oven for about 20 minutes. They should be light brown. Remove; if the circles are not perfectly round, cut the edges while they are still hot (when they become cold, they are difficult to cut without breaking the crust). Cover with foil and keep in a cool spot.

Stop here if you are working ahead.

When you are preparing to serve the cake, make the filling.

Filling:
1 pint heavy cream
1 egg white
1 teaspoon rum
1 teaspoon extra-fine sugar
1 cup fresh or frozen strawberries
Powdered sugar for serving
Extra strawberries for serving
Extra whipped heavy cream for serving

In a small bowl, beat the heavy cream until stiff. In another small bowl beat the egg white until it forms peaks. Fold the beaten egg white into the heavy cream. Add the rum, sugar, and strawberries. Mix well. When ready to serve, sandwich the filling between the rounds of cake. Do not put filling on top of cake.

How to serve:

This cake should be served on a round or square wooden tray. Sprinkle powdered sugar over the top of the cake, and in the middle, put a cluster of fresh strawberries or one large strawberry. Put fresh strawberries around the bottom of the cake and serve extra sweetened whipped heavy cream in a small glass bowl. I dare you to pass this one by!

Knife-and-Fork Buffet Dinners: Menu II

APPETIZERS: Hot Seafood Cocktail
               (Can be done a day ahead)
               Striped Bass in Aspic
               (Can be done a day ahead)

MAIN DISHES: Veal Roll with Bearnaise Sauce
               (Must be done the same day)
               Tongue with Madiera Raisin Sauce and
               Rice Pilaf
               (Can be done a day ahead)
               Fried Chicken Pieces
               (Can be done a day ahead)
               Assorted Vegetables on a Platter
               (Can be done a day ahead)

SALADS: Garden Salads
               (Should be done early the same day)

CHEESE
WITH CRACKERS
AND BREADS   *(Cheese can be bought 2 days ahead)*

DESSERTS: Fruit Ring Cake
               (Can be done a day ahead)
               Chocolate Surprise Cake
               (Can be done a day ahead)

HOT SEAFOOD COCKTAIL
(Can be done a day ahead)   SERVES 8

    1 stick butter (¼ pound)
    ¼ cup chopped onions
    3 medium-sized, chopped green peppers
    ½ teaspoon chopped garlic

2 cans tomato soup
2 pounds raw shrimp
2 pounds rice
Butter
1 pound scallops
2 dozen oysters
Parsley for serving
Lemon slices for serving
½ pound lobster meat (optional)

Melt the butter in a skillet and lightly sauté together the onions, peppers, and garlic until the onions turn slightly yellow. Add the tomato soup. *Do not heat.* Transfer the mixture to a bowl and refrigerate. Cook the shrimp in a saucepan with a half cup of water until they are a little pink. Cool. Save the stock. Shell and devein the shrimp. Refrigerate them and their stock separately.

Stop here if you are working ahead.

When you are preparing to serve, boil the rice until it is tender. Rinse, drain, and put in oven-proof serving dish. Add chips of butter on top and cover with foil. Then place in the oven to keep warm. Put the tomato soup mixture in a large pot and slowly heat it. Add the shrimp stock, and when it is hot but not boiling, add the scallops, oysters, and cooked shrimp. Add more seasoning if necessary. Do not allow the soup to boil, and do not heat for more than 3 minutes.

How to serve:

I like to serve this dish in a shallow, oval copper pan. First put in the hot rice, and then pour the mixture over it. Put parsley and some lemon wedges around it in a wreath. This dish is easy to make, very appetizing to look at, and very tasty. You will want to serve it over and over again.

Special hints: To make this dish even more tasty, I add lobster meat just at the end. Lobster meat cooks very quickly and can be put in at the last minute with the oysters and scallops. If I use lobster, I use the whole shell as a decoration beside the copper pan.

If you don't want the work of preparing fresh shrimp, buy shrimp that have already been cooked and prepared. Then, just put them in the stock at the last minute before serving.

STRIPED BASS IN ASPIC

(Can be done a day ahead)   SERVES 8

This recipe must be done in two parts to allow the fish to cool. Even though it looks difficult, I think the words "time consuming" are better. Read the directions carefully and then have the confidence that you can—and will—make this dish.

Part I:
1 four- to five-pound striped bass
3 pints water
1 quartered lemon
1 quartered onion
1 teaspoon parsley
1 stalk chopped celery
1 large chopped carrot
1 teaspoon salt
1 teaspoon pepper
½ cup white wine
1 teaspoon tarragon

Preheat the oven to 350°. Put striped bass in shallow pan with water, lemon, onion, parsley, celery, carrot, salt, pepper, wine, and tarragon. Simmer gently in the oven, basting every so often. It should be ready in ½ hour. You can tell it is cooked if it is soft when you touch it. Allow it to cool in the pan out of the oven for easy handling. When cool, gently take it out and put it on the serving dish you will be using. Carefully remove the skin; leave the head and tail on. Put to the side where it will cool completely.

Part II:
1 peeled and thinly sliced carrot
1 small thinly sliced turnip
2 or 3 thinly sliced radishes
1 small thinly sliced beet
Black olives
Bunch watercress
2 envelopes plain gelatin
2 tablespoons cold water

2 *tablespoons warmed white wine*
1 *teaspoon lemon juice*
Salt and pepper to taste
Bunch parsley or watercress for serving
Lemon slices for serving

Using the thin slices of raw carrot, turnip, radishes, and beet, make flower shapes. Use the olives for the centers of the flowers and the watercress stems as the stems of the flowers. Arrange around the fish on the platter. Be as creative as you want to be. Try to keep the shapes uniform and not too large.

Soften the gelatin with the cool water in a small bowl, then add the 2 tablespoons of warmed wine to dissolve it. Add the lemon juice and salt and pepper to taste. Spoon the dissolved aspic over the fish and flowers with care. Rearrange the flowers if they are out of shape. Put into the refrigerator until ready to be served with cold mustard sauce.

Cold mustard sauce:
This tasty sauce is a must for cold fish. It also goes well with hard-boiled eggs.

½ *cup mayonnaise (homemade if possible)*
4 *tablespoons Dijon mustard*
Pinch salt
Pinch pepper

Put the mayonnaise, mustard, salt and pepper in a small bowl. Mix with fork until well blended. Taste. Add extras if needed. The sauce should be light brown in color and very tasty.

How to serve:
Aspic fish should always have lemon wedges around it and across its body. For added color, add sprigs of fresh parsley or watercress. The cold mustard sauce should be in a glass bowl next to the fish on your knife-and-fork buffet table.

Special hint: Some people do not like to see the head on the fish, so what I do is put sprigs of parsley or watercress on the neck of the fish. This covers it quite a bit.

VEAL ROLL WITH BEARNAISE SAUCE

(Must be done the same day) SERVES 8

1 tablespoon salt
1 tablespoon pepper
½ clove crushed garlic
1 five-pound cut of boned, rolled veal from the leg
¼ pound sliced bacon
Truffles or mushrooms for serving

Preheat the oven to 350°. Rub the salt, pepper, and crushed garlic on the rolled veal. Place the sliced bacon all over the top and roast in the oven for at least 2 hours. Baste frequently. Take out of the oven and set aside to cool. When cold, put into the refrigerator. Scrape out the pan drippings and put them into a small bowl to save for sauce. Refrigerate.

Stop here if you are working ahead.

At least an hour before your guests arrive, take out the veal and sauce and keep them at room temperature. Begin making the Bearnaise sauce.

Bearnaise sauce:
2 tablespoons butter
3 tablespoons flour
1 cup chicken stock
½ cup light cream
2 tablespoons veal drippings
½ teaspoon tomato paste
Small, crushed clove garlic
2 teaspoons herbs (chives, tarragon)
Truffle or mushrooms (optional)

Melt the butter in a skillet. Remove from the heat and stir in the flour until blended. Put back on the heat and slowly add the stock, stirring all the time until thick. Add the light cream, drippings from the veal pan, tomato paste, crushed garlic, and herbs. Keep stirring the entire time. The sauce will be thick. Taste for seasoning and then put to the side to keep warm.

When the sauce is finished, put the rolled veal into the oven at a moderate temperature (325°), because you are only reheating. Keep in until completely hot, about 30–45 minutes.

How to serve:

When the veal is hot and the guests are ready to eat, carve the veal into ½-inch-thick slices and place on your serving platter, letting the slices overlap each other. Be sure all of the string has been removed. Put the Bearnaise sauce over each slice. The slices should be completely covered. A thin slice of truffle or a big sautéed mushroom on each slice is tasty and eye appealing too.

TONGUE WITH MADEIRA RAISIN SAUCE AND RICE PILAF

(Can be done a day ahead)　　　　　　　　　　　　　　SERVES 8

> *1 four- to five-pound whole cooked beef tongue*
> *1 cup white raisins*
> *1 cup Madeira wine*
> *Chopped parsley for serving*

When you buy the tongue, be sure it is not too fatty. Slice into thin slanted pieces. Put a little wine on it to keep it moist. Wrap in aluminum foil and put into the refrigerator. Soak the raisins in the Madeira wine. While the raisins are soaking, make the Madeira raisin sauce.

Madeira raisin sauce:

> *1 stick butter (¼ pound)*
> *3 tablespoons flour*
> *1½ cups chicken stock*
> *1 teaspoon dry hot mustard*
> *1 teaspoon red currant jelly*
> *½ cup Madeira wine*

Melt the butter in a skillet. Add the flour, stirring the entire time. Slowly add the stock, stirring until thick. Add the mustard, jelly, and Madeira wine. The sauce will be nice and thick. Cool. Put into a small bowl and refrigerate.

Stop here if you are working ahead.

When preparing to serve, take the tongue and sauce out of the refrigerator. Put the sauce into a chafing dish or a large skillet and heat it very slowly. *Do not boil.* If it is still very thick, add some more wine. Add the tongue slices and the raisins in wine to the sauce. Let them blend together in the skillet or chafing dish. Keep at the same heat if possible. Do not let it boil.

How to serve:
This is a nice dish for a chafing dish, but it can be served effectively in an oval copper pan. Chopped parsley sprinkled on top gives added color and does not alter the taste.

Special hint: Use a long-handled spoon for this dish, and be sure you have a spoon rest nearby so that the spoon is not left in the chafing dish or copper pan, where the handle can get hot enough to burn your hands. A plain rice pilaf makes a great combination with Tongue with Madeira Raisin Sauce.

Rice pilaf:
2 tablespoons fat
1 medium-sized sliced onion
1 pound rice
2 teaspoons salt
1 teaspoon pepper
2 cups chicken stock

Put the fat in a heavy pan. Add the onion and cook quickly for about 1 minute. Add the rice, salt, and pepper. Cook very slowly, for about 5 minutes, stirring all the time. Add the chicken stock to ½ inch above rice, cover with wax paper, put on the lid, and cook in a 375° oven for about 25 minutes. Remove and add more seasoning. This is a basic rice pilaf, and can be varied by adding any seasonings, vegetables, or cooked meats you want.

FRIED CHICKEN PIECES

(Can be done a day ahead)   SERVES 8

> *3 two and one-half pound chickens cut into 8 pieces each*
> *1 cup flour*
> *1 cup bread crumbs*
> *2 tablespoons salt*
> *2 tablespoons pepper*
> *1 tablespoon paprika*
> *2 cups vegetable oil*
> *Cranberry jelly for serving*
> *Watercress for serving*

Put the flour, bread crumbs, salt, pepper, and paprika into a medium-sized paper bag. Shake it all up very well and drop in a few pieces of chicken at a time until all the chicken pieces have been well coated. While you are doing this, put the vegetable oil into a large skillet and allow it to get hot. When hot enough for frying, add a few of the coated chicken pieces at a time. Do not pack them in; allow room in the skillet or they will not brown properly. Turn the pieces when they are browned and cook until done. Put the cooked pieces on paper towels to absorb the fat. Cool. Refrigerate.

Stop here if you are working ahead.

About an hour before your guests arrive, take the chicken pieces out of the refrigerator and keep at room temperature. Preheat the oven to 350°. Cover the pieces with foil and put them in the oven for about 15 minutes. Uncover and cook for another 15 minutes to give the chicken that crispy taste.

How to serve:

When preparing to serve, put all the chicken on a large silver platter with cranberry jelly on one end of the platter and watercress on the other. Or, put a checkered cotton napkin in a big shallow basket with folds overlapping the sides, and then put in the pieces of chicken. Make sure the pieces go all the way to the top so that it really looks full. It it doesn't, use either more chicken or a smaller basket the next time. It's delicious and a wonderful conversation piece.

ASSORTED VEGETABLES ON A PLATTER
(Can be done a day ahead) SERVES 8

If you display your vegetables in a nice way, people will eat them. Try this on your buffet table.

1 large head cauliflower
1 pound asparagus (if not in season, try broccoli)
2 bunches medium-sized carrots
2 pounds green string beans
2 pounds small white onions
1 large turnip
Butter
Salt
Sprigs of watercress

Cook the vegetables separately according to their sizes and textures. When they have been cooked, drain and then cut them into the sizes necessary for an attractive platter. Wrap them individually in foil and put them into the refrigerator.

Stop here if you are working ahead.

When preparing to serve, unwrap the vegetables and put some chips of butter on them. Rewrap the vegetables and put them into a moderate oven to heat. When they are as hot as can be, take them out of the oven, sprinkle with a little salt, and start to arrange them on your platter. Think of color, size, and texture. Try the following arrangement and see how you like it: start with asparagus, then the cauliflower, carrots, green beans, small white onions, and then at last, the turnip.

Put some melted butter on them and some sprigs of watercress and see how quickly they will be eaten.

How to serve:
If you have an oven-proof lazy susan, it is perfect to use, since the vegetables stay in the spaces. It's nice also to use a cluster of Pyrex dishes.

Special hint: These vegetables can also be served cold with Sauce Vinaigrette (see page 194).

GARDEN SALADS
(Should be done early the same day) SERVES 8

A fresh salad is always popular. Use everything really fresh and think about contrasts in colors and textures. The vegetables included below make an especially good salad.

Boston lettuce
Escarole
5 tomatoes
3 cucumbers
Sliced scallions
Sliced green and red peppers
Sliced mushrooms
Small bunch fresh radishes
Fresh chopped tarragon
Fresh chopped parsley
French Dressing for serving (see page 192)

After you have sliced the vegetables, keep them in individual bowls until you start setting up your salad pattern.

In a great big salad bowl, line up the Boston lettuce. Then add some escarole on top of the lettuce. In a pattern of colors and textures line up the remaining vegetables (tomatoes, cucumbers, scallions, green and red peppers, mushrooms, and whole red radishes) on the greens. Add the chopped tarragon and parsley. On the side, have some French dressing ready.

Have the guests make their own salad and take as much of the dressing as they want. It's fun and a conversation piece. This dish makes a great buffet table display.

CHEESE WITH CRACKERS AND BREAD
(Cheese can be bought 2 days ahead)

Cheeses are very personal. If you are unfamiliar with them, it is best to trust your cheese man. Heed his advice and buy what he suggests, but it's always sensational to serve a wheel of Brie and a wheel of Port Salut for a buffet table display.

How to serve:

The best way to serve cheese is on plates or in the same thin boxes it came in. Have cheese knives and all kinds of crackers and thin slices of dark bread around. Cheese must be at room temperature when served.

Special hint: If you know your cheese and are serving a lot of varieties, make little name signs for the cheeses. They will become a conversation piece.

FRUIT RING CAKE
(Can be done a day ahead) SERVES 8

½ *cup water*
2 *tablespoons butter*
½ *cup flour*
3 *whole eggs*
½ *teaspoon salt*
1 *whole beaten egg*
Fresh berries
1 *pint whipped heavy cream*
Powdered sugar

Put the water and butter in a saucepan and let it come slowly to a boil. Throw in the flour while boiling. Remove from the heat and beat until smooth. Add the eggs, one at a time, and continue beating. It will take on a shiny look. Add the salt. Set into the refrigerator for ½ hour. Grease jelly roll pan with butter, sprinkle a little flour on it, and mark a 10-inch circle. Put the dough into a pastry bag and go around the drawn circle, making the dough into a ring. Go around again on top of the first circle. Brush with a beaten egg that has had a little water added into it. Put into oven at 350° for at least an hour. It will rise to double its size. When firm to the touch and golden brown, remove from the oven and allow to cool.

Stop here if you are working ahead.

It's best to use fresh berries for this cake. I prefer using a mixture of strawberries and blueberries, but you can use just one kind of berry. Take the berries and clean them. Slice the strawberries in half. Put into the refrigerator. Whip a pint of heavy cream until it is stiff. When preparing to serve, take the cake ring, cut it in half, put the heavy cream on the bottom of the cake, sprinkle the berries all over the cream, put the other half of the cake on top, sprinkle some powdered sugar over it, and place the rest of the fresh berries in a ring around the cake.

How to serve:
Place the cake on a large doily on a pretty plate or wooden tray. Sprinkle some more powdered sugar over the cake. Cut on a slant. Serve with extra whipped cream if desired.

CHOCOLATE SURPRISE CAKE
(Can be done a day ahead)   SERVES 8

1 stick butter (¼ pound)
1¼ cups sugar
3 large eggs
3 cups sifted cake flour
3 teaspoons baking powder
¼ teaspoon salt
1 cup milk (room temperature)
1 tablespoon vanilla
2 cups whipped heavy cream
2 tablespoons powdered sugar

Preheat the oven to 375°. Take out the butter and allow it to soften. Butter lightly a quart melon-shaped mold or springform cake pan, and dust it with flour. Cream together the butter and sugar. Add eggs one at a time, beating the mixture each time until light and fluffy and light yellow in color. Resift the cake flour 3 times with baking powder and salt. Add the flour and milk alternately to the batter. Stir until well blended. Add the vanilla. Stir again.

Pour the batter into the mold or cake pan. Bake for 40 minutes. Test with a toothpick or knife. If it comes out clean, the cake is done. Take it out and allow it to cool. When cool, unmold, turn upside down, and cover with aluminum foil. Now make the icing.

Rich chocolate sauce or icing:

6 ounces semi-sweet dark chocolate
1 tablespoon butter
1 cup sugar
½ pint whipped heavy cream
1 teaspoon almond extract

Melt the chocolate with the butter in the top of the double boiler over hot, not boiling, water. Mix in the sugar and stir until it comes to a boil. Remove from the heat and allow it to cool.

Stop here if you are working ahead.

When you are preparing to serve the cake, cut off the top layer (about 1 inch). Set that piece aside. Whip together the heavy cream and sugar. Scoop out the inside of the cake, leaving a shell about 3 inches thick. Fill the cake with the whipped, sweetened, heavy cream. Replace the top of the cake. Put into the refrigerator and allow to cool while you finish the icing.

Soften the icing chocolate mixture over a little warm water. Beat the heavy cream until it is very stiff and add the almond extract. Remove the chocolate mixture from over the water and fold in the whipped cream.

How to serve:

Serve the cake in a glass bowl. Pour the icing on top of the cake and let it drip down over the sides. Have a separate bowl of whipped heavy cream to serve separately. It is pretty to look at and delicious to taste.

Special hints: You can also put ice cream inside the cake instead of whipped cream. It's a matter of choice. You can also sprinkle the cake heavily with powdered sugar and put swirls of chocolate on the top, but it is best with the rich chocolate icing. You will not be able to supply the seconds requested by your guests!

Knife-and-Fork Buffet Dinners: Menu III

APPETIZERS:	Terrine d' Extraordinaire *(Can be done 3 days ahead)* Prosciutto and Fruit Bowl *(Must be done the same day)*
MAIN DISHES:	Ragout of Beef with Tomato Sauce *(Can be done a day ahead)* Petite Stuffed Veal Rolls *(Can be done a day ahead)* Chicken in Tasty Garlic Sauce *(Can be done a day ahead)*
VEGETABLES:	Golden Cabbage Casserole *(Can be done a day ahead)* Spinach Roll *(Can be done a day ahead)*
DESSERTS:	Plain Cake for Company *(Can be done a day ahead)* Rum Tease Balls *(Can be done 2 days ahead)* Chocolate Cheesecake *(Can be done a day ahead)*

TERRINE D' EXTRAORDINAIRE

(Can be done 3 days ahead)   SERVES 8

The very best restaurants serve a terrine. You should too. You can make it very tasty if you use the right ingredients.

1½ pounds ground, cooked duck, goose, or chicken meat
½ pound pork cubes
½ pound salt pork cubes

½ pound ground veal
2 tablespoons freshly ground pepper
2 tablespoons salt
¼ cup brandy
1 teaspoon ginger
1 teaspoon cinnamon
1 teaspoon ground cloves
2 beaten eggs
4 slices bacon
Sour pickles for serving
Bibb lettuce for serving
Buttered dark bread for serving
Black olives for serving

Put the duck, goose, or chicken—whichever you have decided to use—into a large bowl. Add the pork cubes, salt pork cubes, veal, pepper, salt, and brandy. Marinate for about 4 hours. Then add the ginger, cinnamon, ground cloves, and beaten eggs into the same meat bowl. Mix all very well with your hands or a wooden spoon. Put the mixture into a deep earthenware or terrine dish. Pat it down and put it aside for ½ hour. Set your oven at 350°. Cover the mixture with the bacon and then cover the dish with aluminum foil or its own cover. Place the dish in a shallow pan of hot water and bake it in the oven for at least 1½ hours, or until fat rises to the top and looks quite clear. Take the dish from the oven, remove the cover, and put a flat piece of foil on top and weigh it down with something heavy. Allow the dish to stand until cool. Refrigerate, keeping the weight on top.

How to serve:

I serve this terrine with sour pickles cut into fan shapes. Cut the pickle lengthwise in very thin slices to almost the bottom of the pickle—then just spread it like a fan. Put a scoop of terrine on a leaf of Bibb lettuce on each plate. Add some buttered dark bread, the sour pickles, and a couple of black olives.

PROSCIUTTO AND FRUIT BOWL

(Must be done the same day)   SERVES 8

One of the most refreshing appetizers, whether it is served on a very cold day or on the hottest day of the year, is the Prosciutto and Fruit Bowl. It is pretty to look at and delicious. If you want something light but with substance, try this.

2 large melons (or avocado pears*)
¼ pound thinly cut prosciutto ham
3 large thinly sliced limes
1 large, peeled and thinly cut orange
¼ pound pitted prunes

Cut the melon into slices and place the slices on a glass plate or in a glass bowl. Put the thinly cut prosciutto ham over the slices and put the lime wedges alongside or in the middle. Slice the peeled orange very thin and put the orange slices along the side of melon. Put the prunes here and there on the top. Squeeze a little lime juice around and see how fast it will all be eaten.

* If you cannot find melons in the fruit market, try avocado pears; but be sure that after you remove the pit and the outside skin, you squeeze lemon juice on the pears to keep them from turning brown.

RAGOUT OF BEEF WITH TOMATO SAUCE

(Can be done a day ahead)   SERVES 8

This beef stew is simple to make, but it is tasty and different. It must be made ahead so that the flavors can merge. Since the meat is very tender, you also can use this recipe for a fork-only menu.

3 pounds stewing beef cut into 1-inch squares
3 tablespoons flour
1 stick butter
6 medium-sized quartered onions
1 cup beef or vegetable stock
Pinch of salt and pepper

1 bunch carrots cut into finger strips
24 whole small white onions
1 six-ounce can of tomato paste
1 tablespoon chopped parsley

Dry the beef with paper towels and roll it in the flour. Melt the butter in a large skillet. Brown meat on both sides. Add the quartered onions, and slightly brown them. Add the stock, salt, and pepper. Cover and let simmer for 2 hours. Remove the cover, add the cut-up carrots and small onions, and cook for another 20 minutes. Add the tomato paste. Stir. Taste for seasoning. Put aside to cool. Refrigerate.

Stop here if you are working ahead.

When preparing to serve, put into an attractive casserole dish. Heat, covered, in a moderate oven. Sprinkle chopped parsley on top when you take it hot from the oven.

How to serve:
If you are serving this dish on your buffet table, leave the cover on the casserole until just about the time your guests come up to the table. When you remove the cover, the aroma will be heaven. I serve this dish with big chunks of French bread, buttered and warmed, and rice on the side if you want.

PETITE STUFFED VEAL ROLLS
(Can be done a day ahead)   SERVES 8

I especially like this as a knife-and-fork recipe because it can be made the day before. It's gourmet and tasty.

3 pounds thinly sliced veal cut from leg (ask your butcher to do this)
1 stick butter (¼ pound)
3 medium-sized finely chopped onions
4 tablespoons mixed herbs*

* The mixed herbs can be a mixture of oregano, sage, savory, and basil.

3 shelled and finely chopped hard-boiled eggs
1 teaspoon salt
1 teaspoon pepper
¼ cup hot sherry
2 teaspoons bottled meat glaze
2 teaspoons tomato paste
2 tablespoons potato flour
1½ cups chicken stock
1 bay leaf
1 teaspoon tarragon
1 beaten egg yolk

Put the thin slices of veal between two pieces of wax paper. With a wooden meat mallet or the bottom of a pan, beat until they are even thinner.

Melt the butter in a heavy skillet. Add the onions, herbs, and chopped hard-boiled eggs. Season with salt and pepper. Spread a little of this stuffing on each slice of flattened veal. Roll up and tie with a string. If the roll is large, tie the string on or near the ends— if small, only in the middle. Add a little more butter to the skillet and brown the veal rolls quickly, turning so they cook evenly. Pour on hot sherry and then remove from the heat. Put on plate to cool. Into the same skillet put the meat glaze, tomato paste, and potato flour. Stir until blended. Place on the heat and stir in the stock, cooking slowly. Keep stirring slowly until it is the thickness you want. Add the bay leaf and tarragon. Remove, and when cool enough, put it into a bowl, cover, and refrigerate. Remove the strings from the cooled veal rolls; wrap rolls in foil and refrigerate them also.

Stop here if you are working ahead.

When you are preparing to serve, take the veal rolls, still wrapped in foil, and put into the oven at 350° for about 30 minutes to get hot. Heat the sauce slowly in a saucepan on top of the stove. Do not allow it to boil. Remove and discard the bay leaf. When the meat is hot, grease a shallow dish. Remove the foil and put the veal rolls in a shallow serving dish. Take the sauce off the heat; test for added seasoning, and very slowly beat in the egg yolk. Strain the sauce and then pour it over the veal rolls.

How to serve:

This meat recipe is best with small potato balls or rice. I usually put the veal rolls in a line, rice along the sides and a bouquet of parsley on one end. You can also put fancy toothpicks on them, or a little parsley flower on each. The taste is magnificent and the look is very appealing.

Special hint: For that very fancy party, these can be served on artichoke bottoms, or on grilled eggplant slices. Make sure you have enough sauce so that it does not look dry when it is put on a plate.

CHICKEN IN TASTY GARLIC SAUCE

(Can be done a day ahead)   SERVES 8

2 three-pound chickens
Salt
2 whole cloves
4 quartered onions
1 teaspoon sage
1 teaspoon thyme

1 stick butter (¼ pound)
2 small chopped onions
5 tablespoons flour
1½ cups heavy cream
2 cups chicken stock
2 minced cloves garlic
4 beaten egg yolks

2 tablespoons butter
1 teaspoon salt
1 teaspoon pepper
½ pound mushrooms
½ cup sherry
1 teaspoon paprika
1 pound cooked noodles or rice (optional)
2 tablespoons chopped parsley

Clean the chickens, dry them with paper towels, and then salt them inside and out. Put them into a deep pot and add enough water to cover. Put the cloves into quartered onions. Add the onions, sage, and thyme to the pot. Simmer for 1 hour. The chickens should be tender and juicy, not overcooked. Remove the chickens and put on the side to cool.

Melt the butter in a skillet and add the chopped onions to cook soft. Then add the flour and make a paste. Remove from the heat and slowly add the heavy cream, stirring all the time. Then add the stock. Continue to cook slowly. Do not allow to boil. Stir all the time. Add the minced garlic, remove from the heat, slowly add the beaten egg yolks, cool, and then refrigerate. Wrap the cooled chickens in aluminum foil and refrigerate.

Stop here if you are working ahead.

When you are preparing to serve, remove the skin from the chickens and cut them into the desired pieces. Put butter into a skillet and lightly brown the chicken. Add the salt, pepper, mushrooms, sherry, and paprika. Keep warm and do not allow to boil. Start the noodles or rice, if you are going to serve either. Warm the sauce with the beaten egg yolks in it and slowly add it to the skillet in which you have the chicken. Taste for seasoning.

How to serve:
Be sure to put this chicken into a large but shallow dish to show it off. There should be enough sauce to put some into a small bowl, allowing your guests to put extra sauce on the noodles or rice.

Prepare the noodles or rice the way you like them. They should be placed next to the chicken. Sprinkle the chopped parsley on top of the chicken pieces just before you serve it.

GOLDEN CABBAGE CASSEROLE
(Can be done a day ahead)   SERVES 8

It's surprising to think of cabbage as a buffet table vegetable, but if you try this recipe you will discover that it is great.

1 two-pound head of cabbage, quartered
1 quart water
2 teaspoons salt
1 tablespoon sugar
½ stick butter (⅛ pound)
½ cup flour
1 teaspoon pepper
1½ cups milk
1 cup grated Swiss cheese

Put the quartered cabbage into a large pot with the water, salt, and sugar. Heat to the boiling point and then allow to simmer, with cover on, for ½ hour. Remove from the heat, drain, and put aside. Cover and refrigerate.

Stop here if you are working ahead.

When preparing to serve, keep the cabbage at room temperature. Melt the butter in a skillet. Add the flour and pepper. When blended and thick, add the milk slowly, stirring all the time. When you have added all the milk, take ½ cup of the cheese and mix it all together. Do not allow it to boil. Keep hot and keep stirring so it does not burn on the bottom. Put the cabbage into an oven-proof serving dish and pour the milk-cheese mixture over it. Put into the oven to get very hot.

How to serve:

Choose an oven-proof dish that will withstand the heat and look good on the buffet table. When the cabbage is very hot, sprinkle the rest of the cheese over the top. Put the dish under the broiler, brown slightly (only a minute—watch carefully!), and serve. It will be eaten by everyone.

Special hint: Because cabbage has an odor when it is being cooked, it's best to cook it the day before. Buy white cabbage—the leaves seem to be more tender when cooked.

SPINACH ROLL
(Can be done a day ahead) SERVES 8

This is a tricky recipe, but the effort and energy put into it are worth it. It's tricky because you have to roll it quickly from the jelly roll pan, and it is difficult to keep it warm on a buffet table. However, I can almost guarantee that the Spinach Roll will be eaten before you have to worry about keeping it warm. It is great for a buffet table and very showy at a small dinner party.

3 pounds fresh spinach
¼ cup water
1 teaspoon salt
1 stick butter (¼ pound)
1 medium-sized chopped onion
½ cup flour
½ cup milk
4 separated eggs
¼ cup Parmesan cheese
¼ cup bread crumbs
Mornay Sauce (see page 189—optional)

Preheat the oven to 375°. Grease a jelly roll pan and put wax paper the length of the pan on it. Grease the wax paper, lightly flour it, and put the pan to the side.

Wash the spinach. Put the water, salt, and spinach into a big pot. Cook in boiling water for about 2 minutes. Drain and cool. Put into a blender or through a sieve or food mill. Melt the butter in a skillet and sauté the onion. Take the skillet off the heat while you stir in the flour. Add the milk and put it back on the heat. Allow the mixture to blend and thicken for about 3 minutes and stir with a wooden spoon. Separate the eggs. Beat the yolks with a fork and slowly add them to the milk mixture. Add the cheese. Stir all the time to keep from burning on the bottom of the pot. Add the spinach puree. Put to the side. Beat the egg whites until stiff. Fold the beaten egg whites into the spinach mixture very carefully.

On the already greased and lined jelly roll pan, sprinkle the bread crumbs and spread the spinach mixture. Bake in the 375°

oven for about 30 minutes or until fluffy. Test by putting a toothpick in the middle. If it comes out clean, the dish is cooked.

Have a strip of foil on your work table long enough for the roll. When the spinach is ready, take it out of the oven, loosen the sides by tugging at the wax paper, and then just flip it over onto the foil. Peel the wax paper off and start to roll the spinach. When it's all rolled up, wrap completely with foil and set aside to cool. Refrigerate.

Stop here if you are working ahead.

When you are preparing to serve, heat the roll in the foil in a moderate oven for about ½ hour. Remove the foil, put on a serving dish, and bring to the table. You can serve it plain, put Mornay Sauce on it, or serve the sauce separately.

How to serve:

The spinach roll is most effective on a large silver dish. I put hot Mornay Sauce on the top only and it runs down the sides, making it look very pretty. I then cut it slanted. Nothing else need be used for decoration; it's nice to look at as it is.

PLAIN CAKE FOR COMPANY

(Can be done a day ahead)   SERVES 8

> ½ *pound sweet butter*
> 1 *cup sugar*
> 5 *eggs*
> 1 *cup cornstarch*
> 1 *teaspoon baking powder*
> 1 *cup cake flour*
> 1 *teaspoon almond extract*
> 1 *tablespoon powdered sugar*

Preheat oven to 400°. Take the sweet butter out of the refrigerator and let it soften in a bowl before you put in the sugar. Beat until smooth and very light in color. It takes about 10 minutes with a beater and about double the time if you are using a large fork or whisk. Add 1 egg and mix until well blended. Add only ½ cup of the cornstarch. Blend very well. Add the second egg and blend well. Put the baking powder into the flour. Sift the flour and add half of it to the butter and egg mixture. Blend well. Add 2 more eggs, one at a time, and blend well. Now add the other ½ cup of the cornstarch and blend very well. Add the last egg and blend again. Add the rest of the sifted flour and baking powder and blend again. Add the almond extract and blend again. Grease a cake mold, pour the batter into it, and place in the oven. The cake should bake at least 35 to 40 minutes. When the cake is cooled, remove it from the mold and put it on a cake plate. Let the cake rest awhile before you sprinkle the powdered sugar on it.

Stop here if you are working ahead.

Some people do not like to put powdered sugar on the cake until they are ready to serve it. I do it in two stages: when it is cooled but not yet ready to serve, and then just before it is served. It gives it a double base.

How to serve:
I find this cake prettiest on a rounded wood tray or a very pretty plate. Fresh flowers can be put around it, near it, or even on top of the cake. Daisy heads are especially attractive.

RUM TEASE BALLS
(Can be done 2 days ahead)

This very special dessert is best at holiday time or for some very special occasion. This recipe makes about 8 large balls or 14 small ones.

2 tablespoons cocoa
1 cup powdered sugar
¼ cup rum or bourbon
2 tablespoons maple or light corn syrup
1 cup finely chopped walnuts
2½ cups finely crushed vanilla wafers
3 extra tablespoons powdered sugar

Sift together the cocoa and powdered sugar. Stir in the rum and blend in the syrup. Add the walnuts. Mix well. Add the crushed vanilla wafers and mix well. Take spoonfuls into your hands and roll into balls the size of a Ping-Pong ball or smaller. Now roll the balls in the powdered sugar. Put on a flat dish and refrigerate. Allow to get cold.

Stop here if you are working ahead.

How to serve:
These balls are best put on a compote dish. Your guests can pick them up with their fingers.

CHOCOLATE CHEESECAKE
(Can be done a day ahead)   SERVES 8

Even though this is one of the richest desserts, I try to have it often. It takes just a little wedge or square to satisfy your sweet tooth, and it is delicious beyond description.

½ cup butter
1 pound cream cheese
6 ounces semi-sweet dark chocolate
¼ cup hot strong coffee
2 teaspoons vanilla
2 cups graham cracker crumbs
5 separated eggs
¾ cup sugar
½ teaspoon salt
½ cup heavy cream
2 tablespoons powdered sugar
1 teaspoon almond extract
Chocolate curls for serving (optional)

Preheat the oven to 350°. Take the butter and cream cheese out to soften. Grease a 9-inch springform pan. In the top of a double boiler, melt the chocolate with the coffee and vanilla over hot, not boiling, water. Melt the butter separately.

Mix the graham cracker crumbs and the melted butter together in a large bowl. Then pat the graham cracker crumb mixture onto the bottom and sides of the greased springform pan. Beat the egg yolks with half the sugar until creamy and light yellow in color. Mix the salt, the softened cream cheese, and the cooled chocolate mixture into the beaten yolks. Put to one side. Beat the rest of the sugar with the egg whites until they form peaks. Fold the egg whites into the chocolate mixture.

Pour this mixture into the crumb-lined springform pan and bake for at least an hour. Turn off the oven and let the cake sit inside the oven for ½ hour. Remove and set aside.

Stop here if you are working ahead.

When preparing to serve the cheesecake, whip the heavy cream until it is stiff. Add the powdered sugar and the almond extract. Make rosettes on top of the cake or just put the whipped cream into a small glass bowl with some chocolate curls.

How to serve:

To set this cake off best, put it on white paper doilies on a large round wooden board or tray. The cake should sit in the middle with a bowl of whipped cream next to it for added richness. Simplicity in showing off this dish is important.

9 ℰ

Very Special
Entertaining and the
Brunch Party

In this chapter, I have given my ideas for unusual party entertaining—simple, fun parties that can be given with a minimum of
work and anxiety for the hostess.

Very Special Entertaining: Party I

THE HERO SANDWICH COCKTAIL PARTY
(Can be done a day ahead)   SERVES 25

A movie critic friend of mine had a cocktail party for twenty-
five, and I thought it was a lot of fun because she made it look like
no effort at all. She even admitted it was no effort. Here is what
she did.

There were two help-yourself bars set up with the bottles of
liquor, glasses, ice cubes, soda, quinine water, and water, plus neces-

sary fruits for the drinks. One bar was in the den, the other was in the living room. You could go and help yourself anytime you wanted to. On a table near each bar was a display of diet and regular soft drinks and plenty of glasses.

As for the food, on the table in the living room was a large tray of cheese, crackers, and breads. A huge platter of celery, mushrooms, carrots, and cucumber sticks was near a dip, next to a beautiful enormous head of red cabbage.

The cheese tray and the vegetable platter were removed after about an hour and a half. Then the bartender brought in an enormous, eight-foot-long hero sandwich. Here is what was in the hero sandwich:

Long hero breads, sliced on the side, the end tip cut off to fit the end tip from the other hero until the bread was a total of 8 feet long.
Corned beef slices
Boiled ham slices
Swiss cheese slices
Turkey slices
Cole slaw

The hero was sliced slightly on the diagonal. In a big bowl on the side were all kinds of olives, baby tomatoes, pickles, and peppers to nibble on.

On another card table in a corner of the living room, the dessert and coffee were set up. The coffee was in a pretty coffee pot, as was a pot of tea. The cups and saucers were arranged so they were not all over the table. Sugar, cream, and a small plate for lemon wedges were also placed on this table. A large glass compote dish held cookies and small squares of brownies.

There were just two people to help serve. The bartender was available if you did not want to make your own drink and to bring fresh glasses, empty ashtrays, pick up dirty napkins, and open the door and take your coat when you came in. The maid was in the kitchen making fresh coffee, washing dishes, and keeping general order.

This is a fun party with very little work while it is going on.

Very Special Entertaining: Party II

THE FONDUE PARTY
(Must be done the same day)

Fondue parties are a lot of fun. You must keep them small and the reach from the side of the table to the fondue casserole must be a close one; therefore, it's best to have just four or five at each table. I got this recipe when I was in Switzerland in the village of Gruyère, where they make that great Gruyère cheese.

Remember, too, that fondue gets cold quickly and becomes gummy, so keep it *hot* while you are eating it or waiting for company to sit down.

Small clove crushed garlic
2 pounds grated Gruyère or Emmental cheese (or half and half)
4 tablespoons butter
2 cups dry white wine
¼ cup Kirsch
3 teaspoons potato flour or corn flour
1 small grated nutmeg
Salt and pepper to taste
Pinch bicarbonate of soda
Sour dough French bread

Place the casserole dish over moderate heat; rub the dish with crushed garlic and leave it at the bottom (or remove it, if desired). Add the grated cheese, butter, and white wine. Stir with a wooden spoon until the mixture is hot. In a small cup, stir the Kirsch into the flour. Mix and then add to the cheese mixture. Add the nutmeg, salt, and pepper, and taste. If you want the fondue a little lighter, add the bicarbonate of soda.

162

How to serve:

Serve the fondue hot at the table over an alcohol lamp, electric plate, or chafing dish. Pass a basket of bite-sized sour dough French bread and tell your guests to spear the bread with fondue forks and dip it into the fondue mixture, eating it while it's very hot. Beer is best to drink with fondue.

THE BRUNCH PARTY

Today's entertaining has an emphasis of leisure time and relaxation attached to it and that's good. The hostess can serve an elaborate brunch without going back into the kitchen every few minutes because the following recipes can be done the day before. Brunch served with a flair creates a pleasant mood that lasts throughout the day. Make your brunch party a joyous one—everyone likes to be festive—and whether it is for a few close friends or that important party, do it with style.

If the party is on a holiday, then keep it within that decor; or if it's just on any Sunday, let your imagination guide you in setting the stage. Above all—have a good time at brunch.

The menus that follow are favorites of mine because they are both festive and filling. I find that when you have men as your guests, little crepes or something similar is just not enough for them. I like to have a good balanced menu, one that you can add to or subtract from, depending on your appetite.

The Brunch Party: Menu I

Chilled Mandarin Oranges with Grapes and Melon
(Can be done a day ahead)

Lamb Kidneys with Rice
(Can be done a day ahead)

Hearts of Lettuce Salad with Russian Dressing
(Should be done the same day)

Hot Popovers with Jam
(Can be done a day ahead)

Coffee

CHILLED MANDARIN ORANGES
WITH GRAPES AND MELON

(Can be done a day ahead)   SERVES 8 TO 12

2 large cans Mandarin oranges
2 large melons
2 pounds grapes
Sprigs of mint

Pour the cans of Mandarin oranges into a glass bowl. Scoop the melons with a potato scooper to the size you want. Add the leftover juice of the melon. Put in the grapes.

Put all of this together into the refrigerator and chill.

Stop here if you are working ahead.

When preparing to serve, mix the fruits around with your hand or a large spoon. Add some sprigs of mint on top.

How to serve:

Make sure you have a ladle or a big spoon nearby so that your guests can help themselves. This dish is very refreshing, and it is also very appetizing to look at.

LAMB KIDNEYS WITH RICE

(Can be done a day ahead)   SERVES 8

  1½ *pounds rice*
  2 *cups water*
  3 *teaspoons salt*
  16 *lamb kidneys (veal kidneys can be substituted)*
  3 *medium-sized chopped onions*
  2 *tablespoons butter*
  1 *teaspoon salt*
  ½ *teaspoon pepper*
  Chopped parsley

Cook the rice in the water with 3 teaspoons salt. When tender, rinse and put to the side. Cool and refrigerate.

Remove the fat from the kidneys and split them down the middle. Fry the onions in the butter in a heavy skillet for about a minute and then add the kidneys. Sauté them very quickly for only about 1 minute. Add salt and pepper. Remove the onions and save the sauce from the pan. Put the sauce and onions into a small dish and put aside. Wrap the kidneys in foil and put them into the refrigerator.

Stop here if you are working ahead.

When preparing to serve, run hot water through the rice and put it in a serving dish. Get the skillet hot, put the sauce and the onions into the skillet, and add the kidneys. Sauté very quickly and pour sauce and kidneys on top of rice.

How to serve:

Serve in a chafing dish, shallow oven-proof pan, or a pretty oven-proof dish.

Make sure everything is very hot. You may want to use extra gravy for the rice, so make sure you have enough.

It's nice to sprinkle a little chopped parsley on top of the kidneys as they are sautéing. It adds a little extra zest and helps make them look very fresh.

Special hint: It really doesn't matter whether you make this dish with veal or lamb kidneys. I like both; you and your guests will too.

HEARTS OF LETTUCE SALAD
WITH RUSSIAN DRESSING

(Should be done the same day)   SERVES 8

> *2 large heads lettuce*

Wash the heads of lettuce and dry them with paper towels. Do *not* pull the leaves off. Put into a plastic bag or wrap in foil and put into refrigerator.

Stop here if you are working ahead.

Dressing:
¼ cup mayonnaise
2 tablespoons commercial chili sauce
1 small minced sweet pickle
1 teaspoon salt

Blend the mayonnaise and chili sauce in a small bowl with the minced sweet pickle and salt. Put into the refrigerator. Cut the lettuce into wedges, place on individual serving plates and spoon the dressing over it. Serve.

HOT POPOVERS WITH JAM

(Can be done a day ahead)   SERVES 8

> *1½ cups sifted all-purpose flour*
> *1 teaspoon salt*
> *4 whole eggs*
> *1½ cups milk*
> *½ teaspoon melted butter*
> *Vegetable oil*
> *Jam*
> *Butter*

Preheat the oven to 375°. Put the sifted flour and salt in a big bowl. Add the whole eggs, milk, and the melted butter. Stir and mix until blended, but the mixture does not have to be completely smooth.

Put 8 custard cups in which you have put a little vegetable oil (about a teaspoon each) on a large shallow pan. Use your fingers to make sure the oil moistens the entire custard cup. Add the batter, filling the custard cups ¾ full. Place in the oven and bake at least 45 minutes. Peek in after about 30 minutes. When they are nicely risen and brown, take them out of the oven, and with a pin or the tip of a paring knife, make a tiny opening to allow the steam to escape. When cool, remove from the custard cups and put into a brown paper bag or wrap in foil.

Stop here if you are working ahead.

When you are preparing to serve, put the popovers into a moderate oven, still in the bag or wrapped in foil, for about 10 minutes. They should be very hot. Put them on a long tray or into a basket. Serve.

How to serve:

I serve popovers in a large, long wicker basket. At the end of it, a glass jar of jam and a small glass dish of butter are kept. When a guest takes a popover, he will also help himself to the butter and jam. These are always a big success.

The Brunch Party: Menu II

Pineapple Cubes with Orange Juice Punch
(Should be done the same day)
Charcoal Grilled Polish Sausages
(Can be done a day ahead)
Potato Pancakes à la Connie
(Can be done a day ahead)
Homemade Applesauce
(Can be done a day ahead)
Mike's Buttermilk Doughnuts
(Can be done a day ahead)

PINEAPPLE CUBES WITH ORANGE JUICE PUNCH
(Should be done the same day)   SERVES 8

Large ice square
1 whole fresh pineapple cut into cubes
2 quarts orange juice
Bunch fresh mint
Ginger ale (optional)

Put the ice square in the middle of a large punch bowl. Then cut the fresh pineapple into cubes and put them in the bowl. Pour on the orange juice and let the two flavors marry. Add the fresh mint just before your guests arrive.

How to serve:
Ladle the punch into glass cups, put a sprig of mint on each, and have your guests drink up. This is a most refreshing drink. Give your guests spoons to eat the pineapple with.

Special hint: I like to serve this punch with some ginger ale poured in just after the orange juice is added.

CHARCOAL GRILLED POLISH SAUSAGES

(Can be done a day ahead)   SERVES 8

4 *pounds of Polish sausage*
Spicy mustard for serving
Catsup for serving

The only important thing to remember about Polish sausages is that you should boil your sausages for just a few minutes in a little hot water the day before your Brunch party. Take them out, cool, wrap in foil, and refrigerate.

Stop here if you are working ahead.

About an hour before serving time, take the sausages out of the refrigerator and let them warm to room temperature. If you are going to charcoal broil them on an outdoor grill or if you are going to do them on your broiler grill, remember to cut them down the middle and then cut them to serving size. When they are grilled, you can put them on your serving plate. They will be easy for your guests to handle.

How to serve:
This dish should be served on a large wooden tray. It's nice to have a big jar of hot, spicy mustard plus a big jar of catsup nearby.

POTATO PANCAKES À LA CONNIE

(Can be done a day ahead)   SERVES 8

8 *medium-sized peeled potatoes*
3 *medium-sized onions*
2 *tablespoons lemon juice*
6 *large eggs*
½ *cup matzo meal*
¼ *cup bread flour*
1 *teaspoon salt*
1 *teaspoon pepper*
1 *cup vegetable oil*
Chopped parsley (optional)

Grind or grate the potatoes and onions together. Add the lemon juice so they do not discolor. Squeeze the liquid out of potatoes and discard it. Add the eggs, matzo meal, bread flour, salt, and pepper. Blend thoroughly. Pour ½ cup of oil into a large, heavy skillet, and when the oil is hot, pour in a little of the batter to brown. Then brown the other side, watching carefully so that it does not burn. Repeat until all the batter is used. Make small pancakes, 2 inches in diameter. Use a spatula to put the pancakes on paper towels to drain. Wrap them in foil and refrigerate.

Stop here if you are working ahead.

When preparing to serve, put the pancakes on a large flat pan, taking off the foil so that they will be crispy again. Put into a moderate oven and bake until very hot. Serve with Homemade Applesauce.

Special hint: Potato pancakes are also good if you add a handful of chopped parsley to the batter.

—

HOMEMADE APPLESAUCE
(Can be done a day ahead)
> 5 *pounds cooking apples*
> 1 *cup water*
> 3 *tablespoons sugar*
> 1 *teaspoon cinnamon*
> ½ *teaspoon nutmeg*

Peel, core, and slice the apples. Put them into the pot with the water and sugar. Cook over a moderate heat until the apples become soft and mushy. Do not overcook. When they are soft and mushy, pour them into a large bowl. With a wire whisk mix slowly until all the apples are blended into an applesauce. While still hot, sprinkle the cinnamon and nutmeg on top and allow to cool.

Stop here if you are working ahead.

When preparing to serve, warm the applesauce in the oven for a few minutes.

How to serve:
The applesauce can be served either warmed or very cold. It's a
a matter of choice. It's delicious with the Potato Pancakes à la
Connie.

MIKE'S BUTTERMILK DOUGHNUTS
(Can be done a day ahead)   SERVES 8

7 *egg yolks*
1 *cup sugar*
1 *teaspoon soda*
1 *cup buttermilk*
2 *tablespoons melted butter*
4–4¼ *cups flour*
½ *teaspoon salt*
2 *teaspoons baking powder*
2 *teaspoon cinnamon*
1 *teaspoon freshly grated nutmeg*
Fat for deep frying
Powdered sugar

Beat together the egg yolks and sugar until light yellow in
color. Dissolve the soda in the buttermilk and add to the egg
mixture. Then add the melted butter. Sift the flour, measure, and
then sift half the flour with the salt, baking powder, cinnamon,
and nutmeg. Stir into the egg mixture until blended and smooth.
Add the remaining flour a little at a time until the dough is stiff
enough to roll out. Pour a little flour on a board. Turn out the
dough and roll out to ⅓-inch thickness. Cut the dough with a
floured doughnut cutter and let doughnut shapes stand for at
least 30 minutes to dry out a little. Then start your deep fat frying.
When the fat is hot enough, drop the doughnuts into it. Fry about
3 minutes, or until golden brown on both sides. Drain on paper
towels. Shake on a little powdered sugar and put to the side to
cool. If you want to freeze these, pack them in a tight container
and put into a freezer. If you are making them the day before, wrap
in foil and put to the side.

Stop here if you are working ahead.

Warm the doughnuts in a moderate oven, sprinkle more powdered sugar on them, and serve.

How to serve:

The best way to serve the doughnuts is to pile them in a high pyramid. Sprinkle powdered sugar on thickly. Do the same with the little doughnut "holes." Be sure to have enough paper napkins nearby.

Soup, Salad, and
Dessert Luncheons: Menu I

SOUP: Bouillabaisse Parisienne
            (Can be done a day ahead)
SALAD: Garden Salad
            (Must be done the same day)
DESSERT: Chocolate Refrigerator Cake
            (Can be done a day ahead)

BOUILLABAISSE PARISIENNE
(Can be done a day ahead)   SERVES 8

3 pounds fresh fish (snapper, halibut, and striped bass)
1 two and one-half pound lobster
¼ cup olive oil
4 medium-sized sliced onions
Small bunch sliced leeks
3 peeled and quartered tomatoes
1 medium clove crushed garlic
3 tablespoons chopped parsley
½ teaspoon saffron
1 small bay leaf
1 sprig thyme
3 teaspoons salt
½ teaspoon freshly ground pepper
2 quarts water
1 cup dry white wine
1 loaf sliced and buttered French bread for serving
Lemon slices for serving

Trim, wash, and clean the fish. Cut it into medium-sized pieces.
you are using fresh lobster, wash it and cut it into about 8 pieces.

10 &

Soup, Salad, and Dessert Luncheons

Anywhere and everywhere, soup is a flavorful and nutritious [
of a meal. Soups of endless variety can be prepared from a sin
basic recipe, for it is by the addition of meats, vegetables, fi
and seasonings that soups become individual. An original
delicious soup is a special way of entertaining that can be
clever and interesting. For your next luncheon, try soup, sala
dessert.

When you are trying to make an attractive and origina'
keep in mind the following basic points:

— Be sure all the ingredients are fresh.
— Keep your salads simple.
— Do not fill the bowl so full that the salad falls ou
    is served.
— Always strive for contrast in colors and textures.
— Have the salad well seasoned.
— If you use cooked vegetables in the salad, mak
    are crisp and not overcooked. This way they wi
    color and vitamins.
— Drain your salad properly. Too much dressing
    off with paper towels.

I

Crack the claws and remove the stone bag and black vein. Put the oil into a large heavy pot. Add the onions, leeks, tomatoes, garlic, parsley, saffron, bay leaf, thyme, salt, and pepper. Put the fish and the lobster on top of the vegetables; cover and simmer for about 15 minutes. By then the juices will be extracted. Add the water and wine. Cover and bring to a quick boil. Lower the heat and simmer very gently for at least 15 minutes. Remove and cool. Refrigerate.

Stop here if you are working ahead.

When you are preparing to serve, put everything back into the heavy pot and simmer very gently for at least 1 hour.

How to serve:

Remove the fish and lobster pieces and put on a separate dish. Put the broth and the vegetables together in a large tureen. Cut the French bread into slices. Butter it and let it dry a little. Put it into a deep dish next to the broth. When ready to serve the soup, take a deep individual soup dish, put the slice of bread in it, pour the hot soup over it and then add a piece of fish and a piece of lobster. Nearby you should also have a small dish of sliced lemons. This is superb!

.

GARDEN SALAD

(Must be done the same day) SERVES 8

1 medium-sized head lettuce
1 medium-sized bunch chicory
1 medium-sized bunch escarole
3 large cucumbers
1 bunch radishes
2 medium-sized carrots
1 large sweet red onion
5 medium-sized tomatoes
2 medium-sized green peppers for serving

Clean, wash, and drain all the greens. Crisp in the refrigerator. Break them into bite-sized pieces and put them into a wooden bowl for serving. Take a large cotton or paper towel and dampen it with cold water. Cover the greens and put to the side. Peel the cucumbers and score them with a fork. Cut them into thin slices and put into a bowl. Put them aside, but not in refrigerator. Wash and clean the radishes. Slice thinly. Wash and scrape carrots and slice to the thinness of a dime. Put the radishes and carrots into the bowl of cucumbers. Peel the red onion. Cut it in half and then into very thin slices. Put into a small dish, cover with wax paper or foil, and set aside. Cut the tomatoes into wedges and put them into a small dish.

When preparing to serve, make the following vinegar and oil dressing.

Dressing:
½ cup oil
2 tablespoons vinegar
1 teaspoon salt
½ teaspoon sugar
1 teaspoon dry mustard

Put all of the ingredients into a screw-top jar.

How to serve:
Remove the towel from the greens. Add the cucumbers, radishes, carrots, red onions, and drained tomato wedges. Pour on the dressing and mix all with a salad fork and spoon. Mix until the salad is well moistened but is not dripping with dressing. Sprinkle a little more salt on the salad and mix again. Take the green peppers, cut them into thin slices and put them on as a garnish.

This salad is very nice to look at, and simply delicious!

Helpful hint: I like to mix my salads with my hands—I can feel when I have added enough dressing. If you find you have added too much dressing, do not leave it sitting in the bottom of the bowl. Take a paper towel and absorb it.

CHOCOLATE REFRIGERATOR CAKE
(Can be done a day ahead)   SERVES 8

6 *ounces semi-sweet dark chocolate*
2 *sticks butter (½ pound)*
2 *cups powdered sugar*
4 *separated eggs*
1 *tablespoon vanilla extract*
1 *package ladyfingers*

Melt the chocolate slowly in the top of a double boiler over hot, not boiling, water. Allow to cool. Take the butter out of the refrigerator at least 1 hour ahead of time to soften. Grease a 9-inch springform cake pan. Cream the butter with the powdered sugar. Beat in the egg yolks, add the cooled melted chocolate and the vanilla extract, and beat until well blended. Put to the side and beat the 4 egg whites until they form peaks. Fold the egg whites into the chocolate mixture very carefully but thoroughly. Split the ladyfingers in half and press them against the sides of the springform pan. Save at least two or three ladyfingers. Pour the chocolate mixture into the pan. Crumble the extra ladyfingers and sprinkle them on top of the cake. Refrigerate at least 5 hours—overnight is better still. Do not freeze.

Stop here if you are working ahead.

When preparing to serve, unmold onto a platter.

Frosting:
1 *pint heavy cream*
Powdered sugar
1 *teaspoon vanilla extract*
Crushed walnuts (optional)

Whip the heavy cream with a little powdered sugar and the vanilla extract. Decorate the cake with the whipped cream or just put the cream into a small glass or silver bowl and put to the side of the cake.

How to serve:

This cake is very pretty to look at because of the ladyfingers around it and the whipped cream on top of it. You can also crush some walnuts and sprinkle them on the top. Be sure you put the cake on pretty doilies. Cut small slices because this cake is very rich.

Special hint: To make it easier for yourself, if the ladyfingers do not stick to the springform pan, dip them in a little rum or vanilla extract.

Soup, Salad, and
Dessert Luncheons: Menu II

SOUP: Mary Lou's Garlic Soup
         (Can be done a day ahead)
SALAD: Individual Tomato Slices Salad
         (Should be done the same day)
DESSERT: Papa's Delight Cake
         (Can be done a day ahead)

Here is another soup, salad, and dessert luncheon menu that you will find interesting and delicious. Most of the foods can be prepared the day before, leaving little to do on the day of the party. And as host or hostess, you will find time to be with your guests and still entertain in a nice way.

MARY LOU'S GARLIC SOUP
(Can be done a day ahead)   SERVES 8

Even though this is a hardy soup, you will find that women like it as well as men. It does have garlic in it, but after you add the extra seasonings the garlic seems to disappear.

6 ounces olive oil
2 medium cloves peeled and crushed garlic
4 cups water
2 tablespoons salt
1 tablespoon monosodium glutamate
4 cups chicken stock
8 slices fresh white bread
8 eggs

Put the oil and garlic into a very heavy large pot. Sauté until almost golden brown in color. Add the water, salt, monosodium glutamate, and stock. Let it all simmer for about 3 hours. Check the seasoning. Put into large bowl, cool, and refrigerate.

Stop here if you are working ahead.

When preparing to serve, put the soup back into a large pot and heat until very hot but not boiling. Place a slice of bread in every soup bowl. Put a ladle of the hot soup in the bowl and immediately, on top of the bread, break an egg. The egg will congeal, and the bread will go to the bottom of the bowl.

How to serve:
The way shown above is the only way to serve this soup. It cannot be served at the table unless you have an enormous tureen so that if you put the raw eggs on top they will not overlap each other but float.

This is a most delicious soup. It is different in texture, aroma, and taste.

INDIVIDUAL TOMATO SLICES SALAD
(Should be done the same day)   SERVES 8

> 6 medium to large skinned tomatoes
> 1 four-ounce package of cream cheese
> 1 teaspoon minced onions
> 1 tablespoon minced chives
> 1 teaspoon celery seed
> Small head leafy lettuce
> 8 large black olives

Skin the tomatoes (see page 7). Soften the cream cheese by taking it out of the refrigerator 1 hour before you use it. Put it into small bowl. Add minced onions, chives, and celery seeds. Mix and blend well.

How to serve:
Spread the leaves of lettuce on a flat glass dish. On each leaf put a slice of tomato, spread the cream cheese mixture on it, top with another slice of tomato, and put an olive on the top.

PAPA'S DELIGHT CAKE

(Can be done a day ahead)   SERVES 8

When it comes to a cake dessert, I find this one light, tasty, and very appealing to look at. Try it and see.

½ pound butter
8 separated eggs
1 cup sugar
2 cups flour
3 teaspoons baking powder
1 teaspoon vanilla flavoring
2 teaspoons cream

Preheat the oven to 350°. Soften the butter. Put the butter, egg yolks, and sugar into a bowl. Beat until creamy and light yellow in color. Sift the flour with baking powder and add to the butter-egg mixture. Add the vanilla and cream. Beat the egg whites until they stand in stiff peaks. Fold in the egg whites until blended.

Pour batter into a buttered and floured 9-inch square pan. Bake for 45 minutes. Check and see if the cake is done. Remove if it has finished baking, and allow to cool. This cake can be frozen. I have baked it two days before putting the icing on and have kept it fresh by covering it with foil.

Stop here if you are working ahead.

Topping for cake:
1 cup heavy cream
4 tablespoons sugar
4 tablespoons butter
1 cup shelled pecans or walnuts
1 teaspoon almond flavoring
Powdered sugar for serving

When preparing to serve the cake, make the topping. Put the cream, sugar, and butter in a small pan. Cook over a low heat and keep stirring until it boils. Add the pecans or walnuts either whole or crushed. Cool slightly and add the almond flavoring. Spread on the cake. Put under broiler for about 2 minutes. It's delicious.

How to serve:

What is very nice about this cake is its simplicity. When it is displayed on the table, sprinkle a little powdered sugar on it. Cut into squares or small wedges.

11 ❧
Homemade
Bread and Hot Biscuits

Everyone has his own preference about the breads he enjoys. The same is true of hot biscuits. Since I respect that preference, I am including just two bread recipes and two biscuit recipes. They are my favorites and I hope they will become yours.

HOMEMADE BREAD

(Makes 2 nine-inch loaves)

> 2 cups milk
> 3½ tablespoons butter
> 1 tablespoon salt
> 2 tablespoons sugar
> 1 cake of packaged yeast
> 5½ cups sifted flour

Warm the milk. Add the butter, salt, and sugar. When the milk is lukewarm, dissolve the yeast in it. Pour the milk mixture into a bowl and add the flour half at a time. When blended, put the dough on a floured board and knead it until it is smooth. Shape into a ball. Place in a bowl. Cover with a cloth until the dough rises to twice its size. Grease two bread pans and when the dough has doubled in size, divide in two. Place each half in a greased pan, cover, and let stand for an hour.

Bake at 400° for 30 minutes. Test for doneness by inserting a toothpick. Remove the pan from the oven. Turn out the loaves onto a rack and allow them to cool.

Special hint: The wonderful thing about this recipe is that it can also be used for making individual loaves. When you are having a sit-down party, you can make a small loaf for each table. Served sliced and hot with butter and jam, it is a great treat too.

A special trick of mine is to pat some butter on the crust the minute it comes out of the oven. It makes the crust shiny, and, I think, a little more delicious.

Another special hint is to sprinkle a little cornmeal on the bottom of the greased bread pans. It adds a little something extra to its taste and looks.

OATMEAL BREAD

This is a most unusual bread, and once you've had it, you'll make it often.

(Makes 2 nine-inch loaves)

 2 cups lukewarm milk
 ¼ cup brown sugar
 1 tablespoon salt
 2 tablespoons softened butter
 1 package yeast
 ½ cup water
 5½ cups flour
 2 cups quick-cooking oats

Combine the lukewarm milk, brown sugar, salt, and softened butter. Dissolve the yeast in the water. Add it to the milk-brown sugar mixture. Begin blending some flour and some oats into the milk mixture. Keep doing it until you have used them all up. Turn the dough out onto a lightly floured board, cover it with a cloth, and let it stand for about 15 minutes. Then knead it until smooth. Shape the dough into a ball and place it in a greased bowl. Cover and allow to rise to double in size. Punch down the dough, divide into halves, shape into loaves, and place in greased pans. Cover and allow to rise for 30 minutes. Bake loaves in a 400° oven for 30 to 45 minutes. Cool and turn out onto a wire rack. Slice very thin.

GRANDMA'S BUTTERMILK BISCUITS

2 cups sifted flour
2 teaspoons baking powder
1 teaspoon salt
½ teaspoon baking soda
1 stick butter
1 cup buttermilk

Sift and measure the flour. Add the baking powder, salt, and baking soda and sift again into a mixing bowl. With your fingers, two knives, or a pastry blender, add all the butter except 1 teaspoon and work the dough with butter until it looks like cornmeal. Add the buttermilk slowly to make a soft dough. Turn all of this onto a floured board, knead it for a couple of minutes, and roll or pat out to about a 1-inch thickness. Cut the biscuits the size you want. Put them to the side. Heat the oven to 450°. Dip the biscuit top into the remaining butter before you put it on your baking pan.

Bake the biscuits for about 15 minutes. If you want them crispy, place them far apart; if you want them crispy only on top, put them close together.

My other favorite hot biscuit recipe is for popovers. I find this always a big hit. The recipe for popovers is on page 166.

12 ❧
Sauces and
Salad Dressings

Sauces can make all the difference to a meal—as the French know so well. In the following chapter I list some of the most famous and widely used sauces and salad dressings that I myself use all the time. I also have noted briefly what food each sauce goes best with.

Sauces

BEARNAISE SAUCE

Use for beef, steaks, or roast (see page 138).

CITRUS SAUCE
(Can be done days ahead)   SERVES 8

This is a good sauce to serve with game and goose and sometimes with pork chunks and pork ribs.

1 cup orange juice
½ cup lemon juice
½ cup red currant jelly
½ cup Port wine
½ cup chopped onion
1 teaspoon dry mustard
½ teaspoon ground ginger
Few drops Tabasco sauce
3 tablespoons cornstarch or arrowroot
1 tablespoon chopped orange peel
1 tablespoon chopped lemon peel
Orange swirls and slices for serving
Lemon swirls and slices for serving

Put the orange juice, lemon juice, red currant jelly, Port wine, chopped onion, mustard, ginger, and Tabasco into a saucepan. Simmer very slowly, never allowing it to boil, for at least ½ hour. Strain the sauce. Put some arrowroot or cornstarch into a custard cup and mix it with some hot sauce. Keep adding more cornstarch or arrowroot with hot sauce until you fill the custard cup. Add this mixture to the hot sauce very slowly. Simmer at least 1 hour longer. It will be thick. Never allow it to boil. Just before it has finished cooking, add the orange peel and the lemon peel. Cool. Put into a bowl and store in refrigerator.

Stop here if you are working ahead.

When you are preparing to serve the sauce, reheat it very slowly, making sure it never boils over.

How to serve:
When this sauce is served on the side, I put orange and lemon swirls around it. Sometimes, to be very fancy, between the swirls I have orange and lemon slices.

COLD MUSTARD SAUCE

Serve with ham, cold beef, or hard-boiled eggs (see page 137).

CREAMY CHEESE SAUCE

(Can be done a day ahead)   SERVES 8

This sauce goes with fish, vegetables, or noodles.

2 cups milk
2 tablespoons flour
2 beaten eggs
Pinch nutmeg
1 cup grated Cheddar cheese
Butter
1 cup whipped heavy cream

Put the milk in the top of a double boiler. Stir in the flour, beaten eggs, and nutmeg. Stir constantly until the mixture thickens. Add the grated cheese slowly. Stir until blended and thick. Put into small bowl. Sprinkle little chips of butter on top. Cover with foil and refrigerate.

Stop here if you are working ahead.

When preparing to serve the sauce, remove from the refrigerator and stir with a wooden spoon. At room temperature, add the whipped heavy cream. Serve.

Helpful hint: If you are interested, you can serve Creamy Cheese Sauce hot. Follow the above directions, but do not add the whipped heavy cream. If you do refrigerate it, simply warm it up slowly. If it is too thick, add a little milk. Check for seasoning.

MADEIRA RAISIN SAUCE

Serve Madeira Raisin Sauce with ham or duck (see page 139).

MORNAY SAUCE

(Can be done a day ahead)   SERVES 8

Serve Mornay Sauce with vegetables (like Zucchini and Tomatoes, Baked Kale, or Spinach Roll) and with fish.

4 tablespoons butter
4 tablespoons flour
1 teaspoon salt
1 teaspoon pepper
Pinch of cayenne pepper
¼ cup grated Parmesan cheese
½ cup warmed milk
1 cup light cream (half and half)

Melt the butter in a saucepan. Stir in the flour off the heat and
season with salt, pepper, and cayenne pepper. Blend well and add
the Parmesan cheese and warmed milk. Put the sauce back on heat
and cook it very slowly, stirring all of the time. Allow it to get hot
and thick. Do not let it boil. Put into a small bowl, cool, and then
refrigerate.

Stop here if you are working ahead.

When you are preparing to serve, take the sauce out of the
refrigerator and allow it to warm to room temperature. Then put
the sauce into a small saucepan. Allow it to get hot, stirring carefully. Add the cream and bring almost to boiling point. Serve
immediately.

How to serve:

Sauces are shown off best next to the dishes they are to be
used with. Mornay Sauce can be put into a pretty oven-proof bowl
or dish and kept warm with hot water underneath it. If you put
the sauce on the table, keep your eye on it to see that it stays warm.
It is a good idea to keep a little extra sauce in the kitchen in case
the sauce on the table gets cold. Add a little warmed light cream
to it if it seems to need a lift. Have a spoon next to the sauce and
a small dish to put the spoon on after it has been used.

SAUCE MOUSSELINE

SERVES 8

Serve Sauce Mousseline with hot or cold fish dishes and with boiled vegetables.

1 stick butter
3 beaten egg yolks
1 cup cream
Salt and pepper to taste
Juice of ½ lemon
1 teaspoon chopped parsley

Melt the butter in the top of a double boiler. Slowly add the beaten egg yolks and stir constantly until the sauce thickens. Add to them, a little at a time, the cream, salt and pepper, and the lemon juice. Do not allow to boil. You can keep the sauce warm by putting it into a small bowl and setting the bowl in a small pan of warm water. Stir every so often to keep the sauce from setting. It is a great sauce and worth the extra effort you put into it.

How to serve:
This sauce is worthy of your best sauce boat—display it and you will receive raves. Make sure it is warm all the time.

VELOUTÉ SAUCE

SERVES 8

Serve this sauce with fish.

3 tablespoons butter
2 tablespoons flour
1 cup fish stock*

* Fish stock can be made by getting some bones or maybe the head of a fresh fish from the fish store. Put the bones into water with some seasoning, and after it has been cooked, drain and put into small bowl to cool.

3 tablespoons heavy cream
1 tablespoon chopped chives
Chopped truffle for serving
Chives or tarragon for serving

Melt the butter in a small pot. Take off the heat and add the flour. Stir with a wooden spoon until it's blended and thickened. Put back on the heat and slowly add the fish stock. Then add the heavy cream. Let it get hot, but not boiling. It should be thick, not runny. Remove from the heat and add the chopped chives.

How to serve:
I like to add a little chopped truffle to this. If you do not have truffles, it's nice to add a sprinkling of chives or tarragon.

Salad Dressings

FRENCH DRESSING
(Can be made days ahead)   SERVES 12–18

It is always wise to have homemade dressings ready ahead of time, available whenever you make a fresh salad. Here is a very good French Dressing. You can keep it in a screw-top jar in the refrigerator for at least a couple of weeks. Add the hard-boiled egg only for immediate use, not for storing.

4 teaspoons salt
3 teaspoons freshly ground pepper
2 teaspoons onion salt
2 teaspoons dry hot mustard
1 teaspoon sugar
1 medium-sized crushed garlic

1 tablespoon lemon juice
½ teaspoon Worcestershire Sauce
½ cup vinegar
3 cups oil
1 chopped hard-boiled egg

Put the salt, pepper, onion salt, mustard, sugar, crushed garlic, lemon juice, Worcestershire Sauce, vinegar, and oil into a quart screw-top jar. Be sure that the top is screwed on very tightly, and when your mixed salad greens are ready, just shake the jar thoroughly and the French Dressing is ready. Just before pouring the dressing on the salad, add the chopped hard-boiled egg.

Do not put the dressing on the greens until you are almost ready to serve the salad, or the greens will wilt. Never put salt directly on the salad greens; the salt should be in the dressing. If you like your salads sharper, add the salt, but eat the salad right away. Do not let it stand.

HOMEMADE MAYONNAISE
(Makes 1 quart)

4 egg yolks
1 tablespoon sugar
2 teaspoons salt
2 teaspoons dry mustard
1½ cups salad oil
2 tablespoons vinegar
2 tablespoons lemon juice

Beat the egg yolks in a bowl until they are well mixed. Add the sugar, salt, and mustard. Beat for a few minutes. Add the oil slowly at first, and when it begins to thicken, add a small amount of vinegar. Alternate the vinegar and oil until thick and smooth. Finish by adding the lemon juice.

Helpful hints: Mayonnaise is not difficult to make, and it tastes much better than store-bought. Here are some little hints to help make your Homemade Mayonnaise a success. Make sure the eggs and oil are at room temperature. Add the oil slowly at first—this helps it to blend easily, which is important in making mayonnaise. Use the whole egg if you want to, but the taste will not change, so it is best to just use the yolks.

CURRY MAYONNAISE

(Can be done a day ahead)   SERVES 8

> 1½ cups Homemade Mayonnaise (see previous recipe)
> 2 teaspoons curry powder
> ½ teaspoon dry mustard
> 1 tablespoon chopped onion
> 1 teaspoon salt
> ½ teaspoon pepper

Put the mayonnaise, curry powder, mustard, chopped onion, salt, and pepper into a bowl. Mix very well with a wire whisk. Taste. Add more curry if you like it spicy. Cover and refrigerate.

Stop here if you are working ahead.

When preparing to serve, taste for added seasoning, and mix well again with a wire whisk or fork.

How to serve:
Put into a ceramic or copper bowl.

ANCHOVY MAYONNAISE

(Can be done a day ahead)   SERVES 8

> 1½ cups Homemade Mayonnaise (see page 192)
> 1 two-ounce can flat anchovies, chopped small
> ¼ cup chopped parsley
> 1 teaspoon capers
> 1 tablespoon fresh chopped chives
> 1 teaspoon black pepper

Put the mayonnaise, anchovies, parsley, capers, chives, and pepper into a small bowl. Mix with a wire whisk until well blended. Cover and keep in the refrigerator for a couple of days.

Stop here if you are working ahead.

When preparing to serve, it's best to mix again with wire whisk and taste for seasoning.

How to serve:
A sauce like this is best served in a glass bowl, or if you have a small cream pitcher of glass, use it. It should be either poured or spooned over whatever you find best for this sauce.

SAUCE VINAIGRETTE
(Can be done days ahead)   SERVES 6–8

> 6 tablespoons olive or vegetable oil
> 2½ tablespoons wine vinegar
> 1 teaspoon salt
> ½ teaspoon sugar
> 3 teaspoons of freshly ground pepper

Blend the oil and vinegar in a screw-top jar. Add the salt, sugar, and freshly ground pepper. Taste to see what has to be adjusted or added.

There are variations on this theme:
— Dry mustard gives extra zest for certain salads.
— Basil is great on tomatoes.
— Dill is very good on cucumbers.
— Rosemary is very good on a fruit salad.
— Garlic is delicious on many salads, but it should be crushed and rubbed well into a pinch of salt before being added to the salad.

INDEX

Anchovy Mayonnaise, 193
Appetizers
Aspic Mousse of Salmon, 107
Caviar, Fresh, on Toast Points
with Vodka, 59
Caviar Mousse, 96
Cucumber Mint Soup, Cold, 25
Cucumbered Fish Mousse, 123
Eggs à la Russe, 31
Eggs with Sour Cream and
Vegetables, 121
Gruyère Cheese Teasers, 48
Herring, Marinated, with
Chopped Parsley, 37
Paradise Soup, Cold, 43
Petite Marmite, La, 74
Prosciutto and Fruit Bowl, 149
Roquefort Spread and Hot
Chips, 108
Salmon Mousse, Hot, 52
Sardines au Gratin, 86
Seafood Cocktail, Hot, 134
Shrimp Bisque, Hot, 19
Shrimp Superb, Cold, 122
Soufflé Lobster Supreme, 67
Steak Tartare, 86
Striped Bass in Aspic, 136
Terrine d' Extraordinaire, 147
Vegetables, Raw, 97

Apple Pie, 23
Applesauce, Homemade, 170
Artichoke Bottoms with Pureed
Peas, 70

Bacon and Lettuce Salad, 103
Bar, buffet, setting up the, 82
Bass, Striped, in Aspic, 136
Bean Salad, Green, 91
Bearnaise Sauce, 138
Beef
Filet of, with Truffle Sauce, 70
Filet Strips of, with Herb Butter,
127
Ragout of, with Tomato Sauce,
149
Ragout with Onions, 89
Berry Cheese Pie, 93
Biscuits, Grandma's Buttermilk, 185
Bisque, Hot Shrimp, 19
Black Walnut Fudge Pudding, 77
Bombe, Fresh Berry, 51
Bouillabaisse Parisienne, 174
Bread
Homemade, 183
Oatmeal, 184
Bread Strips, 8, 11
Breast of Veal Farcie, 87
Brunch Party, 163-172

Buffet dinners
  fork-only, 85-119
    menus, 85, 96, 107
  knife-and-fork, 120-159
    menus, 120, 134, 147
Buffet party
  how to run a, 81-84
  purchasing guide for drinks, 83
  setting up the bar, 82
  setting up the table, 81-82
  worksheet list, 82
Butter, Herb, 128
Buttermilk Doughnuts, Mike's, 171

Cabbage, Red, with Apples and
    Raisins, 17
Cabbage Casserole, Golden, 153
Caesar Salad with French Dressing,
    77
Cake
  Chocolate Refrigerator, 177
  Chocolate Surprise, 145
  Cinnamon, 94
  French Strawberry, 131
  Fruit Ring, 144
  Papa's Delight, 181
  Plain, for Company, 156
  Rum Form, 55
  Thousand Leaves, 104
Calendar, entertaining progress,
    13-15
Caneton à L'Orange, 113
Carrot and olive garnish, 8
Carrots with Grapes, 129
Casserole, Golden Cabbage, 153
Caviar, Fresh, on Toast Points with
    Vodka, 59
Caviar Mousse, 96
Cheese, 64, 93
  Assorted, with Grapes, 72
  Baked Kale Gruyère, 114

Fondue Party, 162
Roquefort Spread and Hot
    Chips, 108
  with Crackers and Bread, 143
Cheese Pie, Berry, 93
Cheese Sauce, Creamy, 188
Cheesecake, Chocolate, 158
Chicken
  Breasts of, Continental, 99
  Fricassee with Bread Crumb
      Dumplings, 32
  Fried Pieces, 141
  in Herb Cream, 90
  in Tarragon Cream, 21
  in Tasty Garlic Sauce, 152
  in White Wine, 54
  Lobster and, with Eggs, 100
  Sweet and Spicy, 126
  with Grapes and Vegetables, 44
Chocolate Cheesecake, 159
Chocolate curls, 9, 11
Chocolate Mousse, Cold, 118
Chocolate Refrigerator Cake, 177
Chocolate Roll, 46
Chocolate Sauce, Rich, 146
Chocolate Surprise Cake, 145
Cinnamon Cake, 94
Citrus Sauce, 186
Cocktail, Hot Seafood, 134
Cold Chocolate Mousse, 118
Cold Cucumber Mint Soup, 25
Cold Paradise Soup, 43
Consommé Unique, Hot, 60
Cooking, creative, 6-7
Cooks, shortcuts for, 7-8
Cream Puffs, Baby, with Coffee
    Whipped Cream Filling, 64
Cream Sauce, 22
Creamy Cheese Sauce, 188
Creative Cooking, 6-7
Croutons, 8, 10

Cucumber and Tomato Salad, 22
Cucumber Mint Soup, Cold, 25
Cucumber moons, 7, 10
Cucumber Salad, Spicy, 39
Cucumbered Fish Mousse, 123
Curry Mayonnaise, 193

Dinners
  gourmet, 42-78
  elegant, 58-78
  menus for, 42, 48, 52, 59, 67,
    74
  simple, 19-41
  menus for, 19, 25, 31, 37
  sit-down, 19-78
Doughnuts, Mike's Buttermilk, 171
Drinks, purchasing guide for, 83
Duck
  Caneton à L'Orange, 113
  Supreme, 26
Dumplings, Bread Crumb, 33

Eggs
  à la Russe, 31
  hard-boiled, 7
  poaching, whirlpool method of, 7
  with Sour Cream and
    Vegetables, 121
Entertaining
  buffet party, 81-159
  Progress Calendar, 13-15
  tips for, 6-15
  very special, 160-163
Everything Salad, 92

Filet Strips of Beef with Herb
    Butter, 127
Fish Mousse, Cucumbered, 123
Fondue Party, 162
French Dressing, 191
French Strawberry Cake, 131

Fruit Bowl, Prosciutto and, 149
Fruit Ring Cake, 144
Fruit Tart with Paper-thin Crust,
    72
Fruits, 64, 93
Fudge Pudding, Black Walnut, 77

Garden Salad, 143, 175
Garlic Soup, Mary Lou's, 176
Garnishes, 8-11
Golden Cabbage Casserole, 153
Coq, Le, au Vin Blanc, 54
Grapes, Carrots with, 129
Green Bean Salad, 91
Green Salad, Mixed, 116, 129
Greens, Mixed, with French
    Dressing, 55
Gruyère Cheese Teasers, 48

Ham, Prosciutto, and Fruit Bowl,
    149
Hazelnut Pudding à la Creme, 130
Hearts of Lettuce Salad with
    Russian Dressing, 166
Help for parties, 12
Herb butter, 128
Hero Sandwich, Eight-foot-long,
    161
Herring, Marinated, with Chopped
    Parsley, 37
Hors d'Oeuvres, 11
Hostess, tips for, 12-13
Hot Consommé Unique, 60
Hot Salmon Mousse, 52
Hot Shrimp Bisque, 19

Ice cream
  Lemon, in Lemon Boats, 40
  with Sherbet Mold, 65
Intermezzo, 58, 59, 61, 67, 69, 74,
    75

Kale Gruyère, Baked, 114
Kidneys, Lamb, with Rice, 165
Kitchens, 3

Lamb, Rack of Spring, 75
Lamb Kidneys with Rice, 165
Lemon Ice Cream in Lemon Boats,
    40
Lemon Meringue Pie, 28
Lemon Sherbet, 67, 69, 74
Lemon wedges, 9
Lettuce and Bacon Salad, 103
Lettuce and Tomato Salad, 34
Lettuce Salad (Bibb), with
        Watercress and Cucumbers,
        61
Lettuce Salad, Hearts of, with
        Russian Dressing, 166
Lime Sherbet, 59, 61, 74, 75
Lobster
    and Chicken with Eggs, 100
    Supreme Soufflé, 67
Luncheons, Soup, Salad and
        Dessert, 173-182
    menus, 174, 179

Madeira Raisin Sauce, 139
Mandarin Oranges, Chilled, with
        Grapes and Melon, 164
Marinated Herring with Chopped
        Parsley, 37
Mary Lou's Garlic Soup, 176
Mayonnaise
    Anchovy, 193
    Curry, 193
    Homemade, 192
Meat Loaves en Croute with a
        Spicy Sauce, 111
Meatballs, Cork-shaped, 101
Melon Balls with Mint, 106

Menus
    Brunch Party, 164, 168
    dinner
        buffet, 85, 96, 107, 120, 134,
            147
        gourmet, 42, 48, 52, 59, 67, 74
        simple 19, 25, 31, 37
    luncheon, 174, 179
Mike's Buttermilk Doughnuts, 171
Mixed Green Salad, 116, 129
Mornay Sauce, 189
Mousse
    Aspic, of Salmon, 107
    Caviar, 96
    Chocolate, Cold, 118
    Cucumbered Fish, 123
    Hot Salmon, 52
    Orange, 34
Mousseline Sauce, 190
Mushrooms, 9, 10
Mustard Sauce, Cold, 137

Oatmeal Bread, 184
Olive and carrot garnish, 8
Orange Juice Punch, Pineapple
        Cubes with, 168
Orange Mousse, 34
Orange Sauce, 35
Oranges, Chilled Mandarin, with
        Grapes and Melon, 164

Pancakes, Potato, à la Connie, 169
Papa's Delight Cake, 181
Paradise Soup, Cold, 43
Parsley, 8
Parties
    Brunch, 163-172
        menus, 164, 168
    buffet, see Buffet party
    Fondue, 162
    Hero Sandwich Cocktail, 160

with help, 12
without help, 12
Party Pork Dish, 124
Party timetable, 13-15
Peaches in Blankets, 117
Peas, Pureed, Artichoke Bottoms
    with, 70
Petite Marmite, La, 74
Pheasants, Baby, Stuffed with
    Wild Rice, 61
Pickles, 9
Pie
    Apple, 23
    Lemon Meringue, 28
Pineapple Cubes with Orange Juice
    Punch, 168
Plain Cake for Company, 156
Popovers, Hot, with Jam, 166
Pork Dish, Party, 124
Potage Cressonniére, 53
Potato and Watercress Soup, 53
Potato Pancakes à la Connie, 169
Potatoes Anna, 71
Potatoes Parisienne, 62
Pot-au-Feu, 38
Prosciutto and Fruit Bowl, 149
Pudding
    Black Walnut Fudge, 77
    Hazelnut, à la Creme, 130

Radish roses, 8, 10
Ragout
    Beef
        with Onions, 89
        with Tomato Sauce, 149
    of Veal, 109
Raisin Sauce, Madeira, 139
Raspberry Cheese Pie, 93
Raw Vegetables Appetizer, 97
Red Cabbage with Apples and
    Raisins, 27

Rice Pilaf, 140
Roll, Chocolate, 46
Roquefort Spread and Hot Chips,
    108
Rum Form Cake, 55
Rum Tease Balls, 157

Salad
    Bacon and Lettuce, 103
    Belgian Endive with French
        Dressing, 69
    Bibb Lettuce, with Watercress
        and Cucumbers, 61
    Caesar, with French Dressing, 77
    Cold Vegetable, 115
    Cucumber, Spicy, 39
    Everything, 92
    Garden, 143, 175
    Green Bean, 91
    Hearts of Lettuce, with Russian
        Dressing, 166
    Individual Tomato Slices, 180
    Lettuce and Tomato, 34
    Mixed Green, 116, 129
    Mixed Greens with French
        Dressing, 55
    Romaine, Endive, Cucumber,
        and Watercress, 50
    Spinach, 45
    Tomato and Cucumber, 22
Salad Dressings, 191-194
    French, 191
    Mayonnaise, see Mayonnaise
Salmon, Aspic Mousse of, 107
Salmon Mousse, Hot, 52
Sardines au Gratin, 86
Sauce
    Bearnaise, 138
    Chocolate, Rich, 146
    Citrus, 186

Cream, 22
Creamy Cheese, 188
Madeira Raisin, 139
Mornay, 189
Mousseline, 190
Mustard, Cold, 137
Orange, 35
Velouté, 190
Vinaigrette, 194
Sausages, Polish, Charcoal Grilled, 168
Seafood Cocktail, Hot, 134
Sherbet
Lemon, 67, 69, 74
Lime, 59, 61, 74, 75
Shrimp Superb, Cold, 122
Soufflé Lobster Supreme, 67
Soup
Bouillabaisse Parisienne, 174
Cucumber Mint, Cold, 25
Garlic, Mary Lou's, 179
Hot Consommé Unique, 60
Paradise, Cold, 43
Petite Marmite, La, 74
Watercress and Potato, 53
Spicy Cucumber Salad, 39
Spinach, Puree of, 63
Spinach Roll, 155
Spinach Salad, 45
Steak Tartare, 86
Strawberries, Fresh Berry Bombe, 51
Strawberry Cake, French, 131
Striped Bass in Aspic, 136
Swiss Steak with Vegetables and Potato Balls, 49

Table, buffet, setting up the, 81
Tart, Fruit, with Paper-thin Crust, 72
Terrine d' Extraordinaire, 147
Thousand Leaves Cake, 104
Timetable, party, 13-15
Tomato and Cucumber Salad, 22
Tomato and Lettuce Salad, 34
Tomato Slices Salad, Individual, 180
Tomatoes
cherry, 9, 10
skinning, 7
Zucchini and, 103
Tongue with Madiera Raisin Sauce and Rice Pilaf, 139

Utensils, basic, 3-5

Veal
Breast of, Farcie, 87
Ragout of, 109
Roll with Bearnaise Sauce, 138
Rolls, Petite Stuffed, 150
Vegetable Salad, Cold, 115
Vegetables
Assorted, on a Platter, 142
Raw (appetizer), 97
Velouté Sauce, 190
Vinaigrette Sauce, 194

Walnut, Black, Fudge Pudding, 77
Watercress, 9
Watercress and Potato Soup, 53
Worksheet list, buffet party, 82

Zucchini and Tomatoes, 103